The Intimate Journal

Sketch of George Sand, by Alfred de Musset, 1833

GEORGE SAND

The Intimate Journal

Edited and Translated by Marie Jenney Howe

With a New Chronology of
Her Life and Works

Academy Chicago Publishers

Academy Chicago Publishers
An imprint of Chicago Review Press Incorporated
814 North Franklin Street
Chicago, Illinois 60610

ISBN 9780915864508

First printing 1977

Printed and bound in the United States of America

Library of Congress Cataloging-in-Publication Data

Sand, George, pseud. of Mme. Dudevant, 1804–1876
    The intimate journal of George Sand.

    Translation of Journal intime.
    Reprint of the ed. published by John Day Co., New York.
    1. Sand, George, pseud. of Mme. Dudevant, 1804–1876—

Biography. 2. Novelists, French—19th century—Biography. I.
Howe, Marie Jenney. II. Title.
[PQ2412.A2E5   1977b]   843'.8 [B]   77-18044
ISBN 0-915864-51-7
ISBN 0-915864-50-9 pbk.

To
FOLA LaFOLLETTE

ABOUT THE AUTHOR

MARIE JENNEY HOWE was born in Syracuse, New York. She studied for the ministry at Meadville Theological School, Meadville, Pennsylvania, where she received the degree of Bachelor of Divinity. She was for some time minister of the First Unitarian Church in Des Moines. After her marriage to Frederic C. Howe she was identified with many phases of the woman movement. In campaigns for woman suffrage and on behalf of professional and working women, she has taken a prominent part as speaker and organizer.

Mrs. Howe is the author of *George Sand: The Search for Love.*

CONTENTS

FOREWORD

THE *Journal Intime* binds together three hitherto unpublished collections of George Sand's writings: her journal to Alfred de Musset; the Piffoël journal, composed of conversations between George Sand's masculine and feminine selves; and appended to these, a scrapbook whose dates overlap the two journals. This last compilation includes personal letters, reflections and mementoes which were dear to George Sand.

These three contributions to our intimate knowledge of George Sand are not widely separated in time, as most of the material relates to seven years of her life between the ages of twenty-nine and thirty-six. A page of final comment was added by her at the age of sixty-four.

The Intimate Journal of
GEORGE SAND

NOTES ON THE JOURNAL TO MUSSET

THE journal to Alfred de Musset appears to be a series of letters intended for his reading. But as long as their love affair lasted, George Sand concealed the existence of these letters from the man to whom they were addressed, thereby implying that they were written less for him than for herself. Nor did she hesitate, in the midst of her solitary musing, to change abruptly the objective of her thought or the person to whom she was writing. Often she refers to Musset in the third person while she apostrophizes herself, her editor, or her God.

In form, it was a journal rather than a series of letters that George confided to paper in the silence of night as she waited for her lover in her little apartment at Quai Malaquais. The room in which she wrote was high above the river Seine, overlooking the cathedral of Nôtre-Dame. As she bent over her desk, anyone watching her might have observed that her pale oval face, with the full red lips, high forehead and firm chin, was redeemed from plainness by enormous eyes whose depth and softness held an almost hypnotic power. A closer scrutiny might have revealed that her expression, habitually dreamy and thoughtful, had deepened into melancholy.

Like all sad natures, George Sand responded to gayety in others; and Alfred de Musset was as gay as George was silent, as self-expressive as she was withdrawn. His temperamental needs had led to so many violent scenes between them that their life together had been a daily melodrama. Accustomed as she was to this exciting companionship, his absence left a vacuum which the unhappy woman tried in vain to fill. Musset's pictures hung on her walls, his books and sketches lay on tables and piano, the rooms were full of the illusory image of his presence. For Musset had abandoned her. Yet his desertions had been so frequent and his returns to allegiance so punctual that she could not accept as permanent his apparent change of heart.

When George Sand began her journal the season was late autumn of the year 1834. She had been contemplating a visit to Nohant, her country home, but she lacked the necessary courage to leave the city which contained her lover, and so lingered on, while he laughed at her tenacity.

Musset's two confidants were his brother Paul and his intimate friend Alfred Tattet, a rich and dissipated man about town. These two advisers hated George Sand, and whenever Musset left her in a fit of anger, they tried to prevent him from seeing her again. Fostered by their influence, an estrangement which might have lasted for a few days was prolonged into weeks.

Before the journal in its present form was completed, November dragged on into December, and George, abandoning all hope of reconciliation, at last left Paris for Nohant. In this healthy environment, among her old friends and detached from all reminders of Musset, she tried to recover her normal self. In a letter to Sainte-Beuve written from Nohant late in December, she refers to the trance-like condition from which she has awakened as "a terrible nightmare," and to her exhausted state of mind as "almost idiotic":

"I dream over the past a great deal. I think I am about to give birth to some kind of sentimental novel. I weep and laugh at the same time."

Alfred has sent her an affectionate letter expressing "repentance for his violences." The only reply she sends is one of impersonal sentiment—a leaf from her garden. Upon receiving the leaf, Alfred, equally sentimental but more personal, sends her a lock of his hair. He asks for further interviews.

"He thinks it would do me good to see him, but he is mistaken, for as soon as I see him I shall love him again, and then all my struggles to break away from him will have been in vain."

A few days after this letter the lovesick woman returned to Paris, where her Romeo received her with open arms. The agony began again and continued until March. When, finally, the rupture was decisive, it was George herself who broke the tie that bound her. Without confiding in Musset, she left Paris secretly to avoid a painful scene—a method of escape which has often been found useful by men, but seldom indeed by a woman. Her exit was the more unfeminine as she left the poet living in her apartment where, to express it politely, he had been her guest through the duration of their liaison. There he awaited her as she had so often awaited him, in vain.

Her reason for running away was sheer exhaustion. Musset never disgusted her nor angered her. He merely wore her out.

What kind of man was this poet to whom George Sand gave the supreme love of her life?

Alfred de Musset was fascinating to women, awakening in them the maternal impulse which seems uncontrollably eager to answer the needs of a grown-up spoiled child. Often it happened that women competed for the privilege of protecting the poet from the temptations of his temperament and the hard realities of a cruel world. He in turn accepted their attention and made poetry of their inspiration, meanwhile carefully avoiding marriage and taking infinite pains to shirk responsibility.

Musset hated, feared, idolized and revered women. To him they were angels or vampires. He never saw them as imperfect human beings. Byron was his hero, and to the extent of his ability he frankly imitated the aristocratic libertinism of his ideal. Auguste Préault, the sculptor, called Musset "Mademoiselle Byron." The sobriquet implies not merely lack of hardness and strength, it suggests also the sympathy and intuition which made Musset more lovable than the English poet.

Musset had a dual nature. Weak and vain, he could be mean as a tyrant or appealing as an angel. In his great moments he was so tender and enthusiastic that he seemed sublime. In one of his earlier plays, *Les Caprices de Marianne*, he divided his own personality between two male characters, Octave and Coelio. Octave is frivolous, depraved and cynical. Coelio is an unspoiled youth, romantic and ideal. An inquisitive friend of George Sand once asked her, "Which is Musset himself, Octave or Coelio?" "Both," was her reply.

Of all the women Musset ever fancied, no one was so perfectly adjusted to this dual nature of his as George Sand. She had served an apprenticeship to paradoxical love in relation to her mother, Sophie Dupin. During the impressionable years of childhood Aurore Dupin (George Sand) had been subjected to maternal fondness whose vagaries resembled those of Musset's romantic love. Sophie had petted and punished her little daughter exactly as Alfred adored and repulsed his darling George. In submitting to his caprices, George sank back into emotional habits in which she felt at home. Cruelty combined with kindness spoke to her the first language of love she had ever learned. In her autobiography she has written a description of her mother which, in its emotional reactions, would serve equally well as a portrait of Alfred de Musset.

"She was," says George of her mother, "the most difficult person in the world to get along with. . . . Irascible to the last degree, one had to pretend to be irritated in order to calm her. It was impossible for me to feel anger toward her. Her rages hurt me without ever antagonizing me. I regarded her as an *enfant terrible* who was forever eating out her own heart.

"To pass from one extreme feeling to another, adoring the one you have lately cursed and caressing the one you have just finished injuring, requires a nature of unusual force. Time and again I have seen my mother's anger mount almost to violence, then, suddenly realizing that she had gone to excess, I have seen her burst into tears and exalt almost to adoration the one she had so unjustly crushed."

Not merely his neurotic resemblance to Sophie made George Sand so helplessly in love with Alfred de Musset; the hypnotic attraction he held for her was intensified by the series of frustrations which, in her experience, had taken the place of a normal heart life.

Her father died when she was five years old, and the mother on whom her happiness depended was separated from her at an early age. Instead of possessing two parents, therefore, she had sustained the loss of both. Grief for her mother wounded her spirit, and the wound was never completely healed. The grandmother into whose charge she was given was too old and remote to meet the needs of the heart-hungry child. Loneliness drove her to create an imaginary object of worship. This sublimation of her need of love she named Corambé, and for many years this glorified being was her constant companion. When she began to write, it was Corambé who composed her stories—she merely heard and recorded the words he spoke. During adolescence Aurore Dupin was educated in a convent, where she lived through an excessive religious experience which absorbed and exhausted her emotional energies. Thus for three more years she continued to sublimate love.

Her marriage was a tragedy. The eighteen-year-old mystic with the nature of a poet became the wife of Casimir Dudevant, a commonplace soldier who prided himself on his possession of an obedient, submissive wife. Two years after the birth of her son the young wife fell in love with a young lawyer, Aurélien de Sèze. This infatuation was dutifully suppressed while, like her love for her mother, it was nourished by separation and frequent letters. After six years of unsatisfying affection sent by mail, Sèze grew weary of post-office devotion and showed his disenchantment by discontinuing his letters. Up to this period, therefore, every love of Aurore's life had been blocked.

When she was twenty-seven years old, Aurore Dudevant realized that she had spent nine years of marriage in a devastating devotion to duty. Casimir was notoriously unfaithful. His neglect, his drunkenness, together with the knowledge that he hated her, gave the unhappy woman courage to free herself from an impossible situation. There was no divorce in France in those days, so the alienated wife went to Paris with the ambition to support herself by writing. The writer signed herself George Sand.

This new personality, George Sand, was as different as possible from the conventionally good Aurore who had lived a life of self-effacing virtue. There had been too much obedience to grandmother, mother and husband. The years of discipline had done violence to her being, as a series of illnesses testified. For several years she had suffered from an ailment which her doctors called consumption. Her latest malady had been diagnosed as organic heart disease.

But now George Sand, unlike Madame Dudevant, rebelled against duty and ill-health. The will to happiness was like the bursting of a long-suppressed volcano. The eruption sent her into freedom with an impetus that carried her too far. Part of her assertion of independence was freedom for her long-suppressed love-life. Jules Sandeau, her first lover, proved unfaithful, and a second brief experiment left her disillusioned about love.

It was at this crisis, when the will to happiness seemed dead, that George Sand met Alfred de Musset. In him she believed she had found a nature to mate with her own. Alfred seemed more ardent than George herself. His expressions of idealism were more extravagant than her most fantastic hopes. Intensity, exaltation, the two quests of her spirit, were at last embodied in a living man, and the man was young, beautiful and gifted. In her love for him were concentrated the elements of all the loves she had ever known. The devotion she had given Corambé, the mystic worship she had felt for Christ crucified, the wifely submission she had yielded to Casimir, the suppressed ecstasies she had dreamed for Sèze—all these emotions of a highly sensitized being were relived for Alfred, and interwoven with them was that habit of emotional slavery which she had acquired in childhood at the feet of her selfish, possessive mother.

If George Sand's yearning for ideal love had become a consuming need, it was because each love of her life had been baffled and incomplete. In the exaltation of Musset's angel moods this yearning was satisfied. The happiness he gave her more than compensated for the suffering he caused.

The situation which drove George Sand to unburden her heart as she has done in her journal, is best understood by retracing the steps which led to the erotic crisis called by M. Lovenjoul "the last convulsions of a tragic love."

Alfred de Musset and George Sand met for the first time in June 1833. Both were contributors to the *Revue des Deux Mondes,* of which François Buloz was editor. Buloz it was who introduced the poet to the novelist. Acquaintance between the two romanticists merged into friendship and, after several weeks of companionship, friendship became love. Musset took up his residence in Madame Sand's apartment and, since irregular unions were not unusual in their little world of writers and artists, everyone was interested but no one was shocked.

Musset at this time was a young poet of promise. His naughty ballads, filled with sensuous imagery, had received the attention and praise of a small circle, but in comparison with the widespread acclaim of his later work his laurels were still unwon. Uncertainty as to his ultimate place in the hall of fame left him without the true self-confidence which comes with proved success. George recognized and believed in his genius, and this helped him to believe in himself. He was strengthened by her understanding sympathy, and exhilarated by the novelty of association with a woman of superior mind. At twenty-nine George Sand had already achieved fame. Before she met Musset she had published *Indiana* and *Valentine,* and had completed but not yet published *Lélia.* With the international sensation created by

Lélia she took her place as one of the foremost novelists of her time.

During the months of Alfred's emotional dominance, George's work deteriorated. From June to December she produced nothing to her credit, and her first great reputation began to fail. Romantic passion, however satisfying to her heart, had proved devastating to her work. A trip to Italy was planned in the hope that it would offer both writers the necessary leisure to produce literature and to pay their debts.

On December 12th, 1833, the lovers traveled by stagecoach and boat to Venice, reaching their destination on January 19th. During the long journey Alfred grew weary of George, and on their arrival at the Hotel Danielli he told her that he no longer loved her. The moment the bond between them broke, the influence each had exerted on the other abruptly ceased. The man reverted to his old habits of dissipation, the deserted woman occupied her solitude by resuming her interrupted habits of work.

While they lingered on in Venice, waiting for the much needed funds to take them home, the two inexperienced travelers, like homesick children among strangers, continued to feel dependent on each other. In those days Venice seemed as remote from Paris as China is to-day. No railroad and no telegraph existed to bridge distances, and two weeks were required for a letter to reach them from home. Their isolated situation held the exiles together in spite of their broken romance.

After their estrangement George fell ill, and Alfred, who liked gayety and excitement, neglected her for "several affairs of gallantry." Then their positions changed; Alfred was stricken with "typhoid fever complicated with alcoholism," and George watched over him day and night, until, assisted by the Italian doctor, Piétro Pagello, she saved his life.

Meanwhile the close association between doctor and nurse gave rise to a new romance, the result, on George's part, of hurt pride and wounded love. As soon as Alfred realized that his former sweetheart was bestowing only time and strength on him and was giving her heart to another, he regarded this divided allegiance as treason. Desire, which had died under her devotion, was rekindled by her faithlessness, and jealous rages drove him to drink and wrecked his nerves. George, advised by the doctor, dared not admit to the sick man her new love for fear of retarding his recovery. Thus in action if not in speech she lied to Alfred. This is the lie she dwells upon at such great length in her journal, blaming herself because she was the cause of his suffering.

Pagello was George Sand's master folly. Her entanglement between two men was destructive to her reputation, as after events proved. No matter how much she justified her conduct by an innate sense of freedom, appearances were against her. She had been, in the eyes of the world and in Alfred's eyes, a monster of heartlessness.[1] If Musset's infidelities had seemed to their world deserving of blame, George might have received some sympathy. Or if she had left Musset immediately after their estrangement, instead of staying on to care for him, her conduct would have seemed less inconsistent. But a mixture of bad and good motives had led her into a situation that required explanation, and no explanations were made. When Alfred reappeared in Paris, alone and unhappy, he was considered the victim of a ruthless woman's betrayal of love.

As long as she stayed in Italy with Pagello, Alfred continued to adore George, and George, who was soon disillusioned with "stupid Pagello," had never ceased to regard Alfred with tenderness. On her return to Paris the close relation of the two was renewed with increased fervor. This second stage of their liaison was George Sand's greatest experience of love. Never before and never afterward was she so deeply stirred.

But Alfred, having recovered his sweetheart, ceased to love

[1] In Les Amants de Venise, by Charles Maurras, the most popular of the many books relating the Sand-Musset affair, is the following comment (p. 163) on George Sand: "One is tempted to conclude that this woman was a monster; for what man expects of woman is pity. Of pity she had none." Again (p. 9) Maurras says of George Sand, "She was, in truth, a beautiful monster."

her. Their meetings were spoiled by his accusations and recrimina-
tions. In the beginning of their reunion George wrote after a
stormy scene: "What right have you to ask me questions about
Venice? What did I owe you then? Since I was no longer yours,
I was free to be his, without accounting to you for my actions."
These protestations of innocence aroused uncontrolled fury in
the poet.

Faced by loneliness, George realized she must either lose her
lover or allow him to be in the right. She then took the position
that even if he regarded her as guilty, her lover might forgive
her as she had forgiven him so many times. This appeal fell on
deaf ears. Alfred could not forgive or forget Pagello.

Since Musset was unable to see her side of the argument,
George, for the sake of close accord with him, acquired the habit
of perpetual sympathy. She thought less and less of her own
suffering, more and more of his, until she identified herself with
him, and, during the period in which she wrote her journal, tried
to judge herself through his eyes.

What George Sand unconsciously struggled for in this series
of letters addressed to her lover, herself, and her God, was a cure
for mental sickness. She was suffering from an obsession which
paralyzed her powers of concentration and left her unable to
work, read, amuse herself, or talk impersonally with her friends.
She had ceased to be a normal human being. She no longer led a
normal human life.

The modern psychiatrist sometimes advises a patient to write
down the whole confusion of his thoughts and feelings without
judging or revising the emotions transcribed. This practice is
supposed to secure relief from psychic disturbance, acting as
drainage for the turgid upheavals of the inner life. George Sand,
long before this method was advised, followed it instinctively.
Her journal to Alfred is her attempt to analyze the conflict which
was devastating her life. Was he right or was she right? The ques-

tion agitated her being. When she identifies herself with Alfred she takes on the man's point of view and condemns the woman. When she is conscious of herself as George she defends herself vigorously against the man who is her judge, only to forget herself again in Alfred and once more see the situation through his eyes. Consciously, she rejects herself for Alfred, but subconsciously the self in her persists and demands recognition.

At times she stands outside the controversy and allows the hero and heroine of the journal to speak for themselves, exactly as George Sand, writer of fiction, allowed her characters to express themselves. The habit of authorship is strong upon her. It is interesting to observe that when she sides with Alfred her writing is often artificial and her tone unconvincing, but as soon as she speaks for herself, conviction flows from the bottom of her heart, and her writing is natural and sincere.

How forced is the language in which she suggests cutting off her hand to win back Alfred's love and forgiveness! And what could be more spontaneous than the moving description of herself between the two men who desired her, and the concluding sigh of self-pity, "Poor woman, it was then she should have died!"

When George Sand was normal she did her work. Whenever she lost her poise she wrote a journal. This manifestation of pent-up feeling seeking relief repeated itself several times in her life. Occasionally, as substitute for self-communion, the outlet was a long confidential letter to a friend. In either case the psychology was the same. When her emotions upset her life she got rid of them in writing, and these outpourings testify how much inner rebellion the tremendous personality which was George Sand had to contend with, in order to do a man's work in the world.

MARIE JENNEY HOWE

December, 1928
Harmon-on-Hudson

PREFACE

THERE are times when a woman, especially a celebrated woman, ought to defend herself against calumny. But to do this she must know how to hit back and, if necessary, hit hard enough to hurt. George Sand knew only how to admire, praise, pardon and love.

After her legal separation from her husband—to-day it would be a divorce—life gave her freedom and independence; for these she often paid an excessive price.

Her courage and candor were exceptional, and her novels were filled with theories far in advance of her times. Thus many people were led to form false opinions about her, even to the extent of injuring her reputation. She disdained explanations and would not stoop to self-defense. But when she was at fault her love of truth and justice impelled her to accuse herself and confess whatever wrong she had done. She met outrageous criticism and hatred by frankness and fundamental honesty that proved the nobility of her nature.

Digging up the remains of great men and women in order to defame their memories is a regrettable practice which continues to be popular. It will pass. Some day the reader, disdaining omissions and distortions that change the face of history, will seek the truth about human hearts that have loved and suffered, and will find that truth in those hearts themselves.

The following pages were given us by M. Spoelberch de Lovenjoul. The manuscript is only a copy of the original, which has been destroyed or lost. Spoelberch believed that this copy had been made, or at least preserved, by Ursule, the Berrichonne childhood friend about whom George Sand has written in *l'Histoire de ma Vie.* I do not know whether this hypothesis is well founded nor on what ground it was based by the erudite collector.

This journal, revealing as it does one of the most unhappy phases of the love affair of George Sand and Alfred de Musset, is the expression of a suffering heart and a lofty spirit.

May admirers of these two lovers read with sympathy what is written in this journal. Let them also read the complete correspondence between the two writers. There they will find the truth, untouched by literary intermediaries who so often misinterpret states of consciousness which they cannot understand.

AURORE SAND

Journal to
ALFRED DE MUSSET

I

At night, from Saturday to Sunday

Paris, November, 1834.

YOU do not love me. You do not love me any more. I cannot blind myself to the truth. Last evening while we were together I was feeling very ill. As soon as you noticed it you went away. No doubt it was right to leave me, because you were tired last night. But to-day, not one word. You have not even sent to inquire about me. I hoped for you, waited for you, minute by minute, from eleven in the morning until midnight. What a day! Every ring of the bell made me leap to my feet. Thank God I have heart disease. If only I could die! You love me with your senses more than ever before. And I you. I have never loved anyone, I have never loved you, in this way.

But I love you also with my whole being—and you do not even feel friendship for me. I wrote to you early this evening. You have not answered my note. They told my messenger you had gone out; yet you did not come to see me for even five minutes. You must have returned very late. Great heavens! Where were you all evening? Alas, all is over between us. You no longer love me at all.

If I stay on here I shall seem to you abject, odious. Yes, you really want me to leave. Only the other night you smiled and looked incredulous when you said, "Bah! you won't go away." Are you in such a hurry to say good-by? Don't be disturbed. I am leaving in four days and we shall never see each other again. Forgive me for having made you suffer; you are amply avenged; no one in the world is more wretched than I am.

Paris, Tuesday evening, November 25, 1834.

I went to the opera [Les Italiens, now the Opéra-Comique] where I made the acquaintance of that nice chap Delécluze. It was the first performance of Ernani—stupid, boresome! Buloz [editor of the *Revue des Deux Mondes*] sleeps at the opera as comfortably as in his own bed. People tread on his coat-tails, they step on his hat, on his feet. He awakes long enough to exclaim "Good Lord!" then goes back to sleep again.

As for me, unfortunate boy that I am, they all stare at me, then somebody says, "Look, isn't that George Sand? Let me see! Show her to me! Where is she?" "Ah!" I heard an old lady say, "she really appears quite decent in spite of everything." A profound diplomat—judging by his waistcoat—looked at me through his lorgnon and remarked, "Heavens, how pretty she is!" A week ago I would have been charmed to hear this. But now what difference does it make? There is no one in the world whose praise gives me the slightest pleasure.

This morning I posed for Delacroix. While we talked I smoked his delicious cigarettes. He gave me some. If only I could send them to you, dear child, they might give you a moment's pleasure. But I dare not. Delacroix showed me the de Goya collection. While we discussed the paintings he talked about Alfred and told me that Alfred might have become a great painter if he had so desired. I believe it is true. The great Delacroix would like to copy the little sketches in Alfred's album.

As for me, I am going to amuse myself—amuse myself?—occupy myself by slavishly copying some of de Goya's pretty women. I shall send them to my poor darling when I leave. Perhaps he will not refuse them. I know he likes such women. If I could take one of those faces, make it my own, then go through the night until I found him! He would not recognize wretched George, and he would love me if only for an hour.

No, I cannot get over it! Well, then, I must learn to endure it. Dear God, do as you will with me. I was talking of my suffering to Delacroix this morning—for I can talk of nothing else—and he gave me some good advice—it was, *not* to have courage. "Let yourself go," he said. "When I am in that condition I have no pride. I was not born a Roman. I abandon myself to despair. It grips me, overpowers me and gnaws at my vitals. When it has had enough it grows exhausted and leaves me in peace."

Will my despair ever leave me? It grows stronger day by day. The heart that used to be open to mine is now wholly closed to me.—Oh, this terror of loneliness!

Sometimes I am tempted to go to his house and pull on his door bell until the cord breaks. Sometimes I imagine myself lying down outside his door waiting for him to come out. I would like to fall at his feet—no, not at his feet, that would be madness—but I would like to throw myself into his arms and cry out, "Why do you deny your love for me? You do love me!"

Yes, you still love me, but you are ashamed of it. You love me and it makes you suffer. You pity me too much not to love me.

Alfred, you know that I love you, that I cannot love anyone but you. Kiss me, do not argue, say sweet things to me, caress me, because you do find me attractive, in spite of my short hair, in spite of the wrinkles that have come on my cheeks during these last few days. And then, when you are exhausted with emotion and feel irritation returning, treat me badly, send me away, but not with those dreadful words, *the last time.*

I will suffer as much as you wish, but let me go to you sometimes, if only once a week, for the sake of the tears, the kisses, which bring me back to life.

You cannot! How tired you are of me and how quickly you have recovered from your love. Surely I am suffering greater wrongs than any you suffered on my account in Venice when I consoled myself. At that time you did not love me, and reason, egotistic and proud, said to me, "You are doing right." Now you insist that I was guilty. But, my dear, all that belongs to the past. The present is still good and beautiful.

I love you. To be loved by you I would submit myself to any torture. Yet you leave me! Poor soul, you are crazy . . . Pride masters you. Of course you ought to have some pride, and yours is beautiful because you have a beautiful soul. But if only you would let reason silence pride it would say to you, "Love this poor woman; you know now that you will not love her too much, so what are you afraid of? She will not be exacting, poor thing. Of two lovers, whichever loves least, suffers least. This then is the very time to love her."

He is wrong. Is he not wrong, my God, wrong to leave me now when my soul is purified and, for the first time, my strong will has lost its power? Is it my will that is broken? I do not know and I am content to remain ignorant. What do I care about their theories and social principles! I feel, that is all. I love. The force of my love would carry me to the ends of the earth. But no one wants it! . . . You say, "One cannot love two men at the same time." Nevertheless that was what happened to me. It happened once but it will not happen again. You are crazy when you say, "She will do it to-morrow because she did it yesterday!" You ought to say just the opposite. Am I stupid or insensitive? Do I not suffer from my follies and mistakes? Are lessons of no value to women like me? Am I not thirty years old and in full possession of all my powers? Yes, God in heaven, I feel that I am. I am still able to make a man happy and proud if he is willing to help me. I need a steady arm to uphold me, a heart without vanity to receive and sustain me. If I had ever found such a man I should not be where I am now. But these masterful men are like gnarled oaks whose exterior is repellent.

And you, poet, lovely flower, your fragrance intoxicated me, poisoned me. You were too suave, too subtle. When I tried to draw near, you dissolved into air before my lips could touch you. You are like those blossomy shrubs of India and China that bend with the slightest wind. From their frail stems we never obtain strong beams with which to build homes. We taste their nectar, we grow heady with their perfume, under their influence we fall asleep and die.

Then, too, I dislike powerful men because they are brutal. I hate their cowardice and hypocrisy. I hate their smugness. They build a whole system of virtue on their theory of crime. But one may commit a crime unconsciously. Whether an action is praised as holy or condemned as horrible is often determined by the after effect, or it may be decided by chance. I once saw an unhappy girl fall on her knees after she had killed her baby and cry out, "My God, I thank Thee for having given me courage to kill this poor little creature, destined to endure so much suffering if she had lived." She mounted the scaffold with the feelings of a martyr.

Preach your big words, then, and make your phrases! Make some yourself, unhappy woman. You who write, unconscious of what you are writing. You who know nothing, nothing, except that you love enough to die of love.

Friday.

Liszt said to me to-day that God alone deserves to be loved. It may be true, but when one has loved a man it is very difficult to love God. It is so different. Liszt said also that the only keen sympathy he had ever felt was for M. Lamennais, and he added that earthly love would never get possession of him.

He is very lucky, the good little Christian!

I saw Henri [Heine] this morning. He told me that we love with the head and senses and that the heart counts for very little in love. I saw Mme. Allart at two o'clock. She told me that we must use stratagem with men and pretend to be angry in order to get them back. Of them all, Sainte-Beuve alone refrained from hurting me with foolish words. I asked him the meaning of love and he answered, "It means tears; if you weep, you love."

Yes, dear friend, I love. In vain do I summon anger to my aid. I love, I shall die of it, unless God works a miracle to save me.

Perhaps he will give me back my ambition to write or my devotion to religion. I ought to go seek out Sister Martha.

Midnight.

I cannot work. Oh, loneliness, loneliness! I can neither write nor pray. Sainte-Beuve says I need distraction. With whom? What do all these people amount to? When they have talked for an hour about things I don't care about, they disappear. They are merely shadows that come and go. I remain alone, alone forever. I want to kill myself. And who has the right to prevent me?

Oh, my poor children, how miserable your mother is!

[On the day the events of which are narrated above—the day on which she went to the opera and posed for her portrait—George Sand wrote to Sainte-Beuve:

"I go out. I seek distraction. I try to rouse myself, keep going. But when I come back to my room in the evening I go crazy—

"Yesterday it was as though my legs carried me in spite of myself. I went to his house. Happily I did not find him in. I could not have lived through an interview—

"His injustice devours my heart. Not one word, not a sign of remembrance. He grows impatient and laughs because I do not leave. You had better advise me to kill myself. There is nothing else to do.

"Do come and see me to-day at four o'clock, or to-morrow at the same hour. I have an appointment with Delacroix for that portrait for the *Revue* and I do not want to stay at home in the evening. I would rather play dominoes in a café than spend an hour after dinner in my own house at the risk of being alone. Alone—what horror!"

Sainte-Beuve was George Sand's intimate friend and confidant. He was also Musset's friend. Disturbed by their estrangement, he tried at first to act as peacemaker, but George's morbid state convinced him it was better for the lovers to separate. He then called on Musset and left a note advising the poet not to see "the person whose distress I have just witnessed." When Alfred returned and found the carefully phrased note in which no names were mentioned, he sent Sainte-Beuve the following reply:

"Madame Sand is perfectly aware of my present intentions. If it is she who asked you to tell me not to see her again, I fail to understand by what motive she made such a request, since only last evening I positively refused to receive her in my house—

"If you let me believe that in order to see you I must quarrel with my mistress, you will force me to be cruel."

Musset's proud assurance that he would not receive Madame Sand is in strange contrast to a letter he had sent her a short time earlier. In this letter, written when he was ill, he had begged her to come and nurse him. When she applied for admission as nurse the door had been opened with alacrity, but now that she went to him in need of healing she found the door firmly closed.

However, a few days after his haughty letter to Sainte-Beuve Musset received Madame Sand once more, and the consequences of this call proved disastrous for George. The following pages indicate that she was baffled by the discovery that others had been told of this secret visit. Her account bears internal evidence that although she insisted on trusting Musset, she sometimes found it difficult to suppress her half-conscious suspicion that he might not be wholly trustworthy, after all.]

II

I HAVE just come from the opera. I was bored to death. I have been depressed all day. Boucoiran read me something from M. de Maistre. Of all he read to me I only remember these three lines: "There are provinces in India where people often pledge themselves to commit suicide in return for favorable answers to their prayers. Those who have made this pledge throw themselves from a rock called—"

Oh, God, God, if you would give me back a single day of the happiness you have taken from me, I would willingly fulfill this pledge; but I shall die without recapturing my lost happiness!

Decidedly music is bad for me and the theatre bores me. People who go to the theatre look so stupid. They appear tranquil but indifferent. Some of them seem happy. While I who sit beside them feel a viper eating at my heart. There I sit alone, wearing my *bousingot*,[1] distressed at finding myself in the midst of all those men in black. I also am in mourning. My hair is cut off,[2] there are dark circles under my eyes, my cheeks have grown hollow. I look dull and old. Above me are all those blond women, white and pink, decked out with jewels and feathers, wearing their hair in luxuriant curls, carrying bouquets, displaying naked shoulders. And I, what am I, poor George?

Yes, there above me is the field where Fantasio[3] will go to select his next flower. Wretched man, why is it that you cannot

[1] A sailor-hat called *bousingot* after the Admiral of that name.

[2] George Sand cut off her hair and sent it to Musset in a desperate effort to melt his frozen heart. This was a lovely example of the romanticism then in vogue.

[3] "Fantasio" is the title of Musset's comedy written in 1834. Musset is here identified with his hero. As she sat in the parterre of the theatre, George looked at the boxes filled with beautiful women who seemed to her like lilies and roses. Obsessed as she was by thoughts of Alfred she felt a foreboding that from among those flower-like women Alfred would choose his next love.

love me? According to logic, according to man's justice, no doubt this is right. But you, my God, my God, you know whether any of those women will ever love him as I am loving him now!

Madman, you are leaving me in the most beautiful mood of my life, in the phase of my love that is most real, most passionate, and most replete with suffering!

You have broken a woman's pride. You have thrown her at your feet. Does this mean nothing to you? Does it mean nothing to know she is dying?—But he does not know.—

You lie, you know you lie, and you are ruthless, when you accuse me of acting a part. Why should I do so? If I cared about what people say, I would have gone away long ago, because I can trust you to defend me. Am I not sure of your honor?

If I left Paris they would only say that I had lost my head, and you, Alfred, would, I am sure, protect me from criticism. That would be less humiliating for me than to remain here and give all those beautiful women the right to say that I disguise myself as a man in order to go to your room at night and crawl on my knees to you. Who, then, has spread this news so quickly? Surely it was not you. Would you hold me up to ridicule before those women? No. But how explain their contempt, their mocking laughter! I was told that at Delphine Gay's [1] all these women were saying mean things about me, and that he answered, "Perhaps you are not wholly in the wrong." But you, Alfred, wrote to me when I was in Italy, "Crow, my fine cocks; you will never make me deny Jesus!" [2] Oh, those letters which I no longer pos-

---

[1] A contemporary woman writer of some repute, whose salon was a center of fashion.

[2] In their published correspondence the complete paragraph in the letter from Alfred de Musset to George Sand reads as follows:

"'Tell me, is it true that Madame Sand is an adorable woman?' This question was asked me the other day by a pretty idiot. The dear creature repeated it no less than three times. She evidently wanted to see whether my answers would vary.

"Crow, my fine cock! I said to myself. You will not make Saint Peter deny—"

In the published correspondence the last word has been crossed out. If George Sand deleted it—and it was she who went over the letters before they were consigned to a friend for publication—it may be assumed that she would have made the same deletion in her journal when, later on, she compares Musset to Jesus, if she had known it would be published. Both these writers, like other picturesque Romanticists, indulged in the exaggerated literary style then in vogue. It must be borne in mind also that in George Sand's journal we are reading the

sess, letters which I wept over, kissed, pressed against my heart when *the other* was not looking! I loved them so, and now I have them no more.

In one of those letters he said to me, "But even if you had lied to me from start to finish, you did not betray me, because we were estranged and you made no profession of love for me." [1] He made a distinction then between women who betray and those who lie. But afterwards he devolped a theory which justified him in showing me no leniency. He argued that I had made no profession of love for him because he [Alfred] might have boasted to *the other* [Pagello], "She has given herself to me again." Yes, he accused me of that.

God, thou knowest whether I could harbor such a thought and whether I ever in my life stooped to such meanness! Thou knowest whether I ever told any other lies! [than those to save Alfred from suffering] Dear God, why didst thou put me in such a horrible position, where it was necessary to lie or to kill a man by telling the truth? Why didst thou not protect me from such danger, when reason, consciousness, life itself hung in the balance? Thou knowest what we poor human beings are. Why dost thou allow us to lose ourselves and destroy ourselves? Thou alone canst absolve me from my failures and mistakes, because human understanding finds whatever it wants to find. Thou alone knowest the truth. Thou alone canst console and restore me.

Then kill me quickly, cruel Master! Have I not expiated enough? I lived through long weeks of terror and trembling. The lies I told seared my lips like a red-hot iron. Again and again I fell on my knees in those frozen churches and prayed frantically

hasty scribbling of a woman who was never given the opportunity to edit her manuscript, and who had no suspicion that her private communion with her lover would ever be read by anyone else.

[1] The complete quotation from Musset's letter reads:

"But even if all my suspicions had been true, in what way did you deceive me? Were you professing love for me at that time? Was I not warned? Did I have any rights? O my dear child, when you loved me did you ever deceive me? What cause for reproach did I ever have in the seven months during which I saw you every day? A man would be a miserable coward if he called a woman perfidious when she respected him enough to tell him that her love for him had ceased."

while my teeth were chattering with cold. And the other evening at Saint-Sulpice, when I cried out to thee, "Wilt thou abandon me? Wilt thou punish me to the utmost limit? Will nothing appease thee?"—a voice in the depths of my heart answered, "Confess, confess and die."

Alas, I did confess the next day, but it was too late. And I could not die, because we do not die of anguish, we live on. We continue to suffer. We drink the cup drop by drop. All night long we are nourished by bitterness and tears, and toward morning we fall asleep, stupefied, only to be harassed by frightful dreams.

Last night I dreamed that he was beside me, that he embraced me. I awoke swooning with joy. What a dream, my God! This death's-head beside me, and this gloomy room where he will never set foot again, this bed where he will sleep no more! I could not keep from crying out. Poor Sophie [her maid], what nights I give her!

I cannot suffer like this! And all for nothing. I am thirty years old, I am still beautiful—at least I should regain my looks if I could stop crying. I am surrounded by men who are more worth while than I am, and who nevertheless would gladly offer me their companionship; men who are ready to take me just as I am, without lies, without coquetry. They would take me after hearing the confession of all my faults.

If I could only make myself love someone. My God, give me back the fierce vigor I had in Venice! Give back the instinctive love of life that seized me like an access of rage in the midst of overwhelming despair. Let me love again. Oh, this man finds it amusing to tear me in pieces. He takes pleasure in my anguish. He drinks my tears and laughs. Then let me die.

No, no, I do not want to die. I want to love. I want to be young again, I want to live! But all these warm impulses have fallen into ashes. God, why did you abandon me? Did I commit a crime? Is the love of life a crime? A man comes to a woman and says: "You are deserted, scorned, cast out, trampled under foot; you may have deserved all this. You have told me nothing about your past. I do not know you, but I realize your suffering and I love you. My one desire is to devote myself to you. Console yourself, live. I long to save you. I will help you fulfill your duty toward this sick man; you will follow him to his destination [Paris] but you will cease to love him and you will return to me. I believe in you." If a man comes to a woman talking like that, should it seem culpable to her? And if—carried away by the impatience of his senses, or by the desire to assure himself of her faith—he overwhelms her with caresses, with tears; if he is first bold, then humble, as he tries to take her senses by surprise? Ah, you do not know what it is to be adored and persecuted and implored for hours on end! Some men have never done this, have never obstinately laid siege to a woman. Prouder, more delicate, they have used persuasion and they have waited to succeed. As for me, the only men I had met wanted a woman to give herself. That Italian! God knows why his first word did not draw from me a cry of horror! And why did I yield, why, why? Do I know? I know that you have broken me because of him, and that for my involuntary crime you have punished me as human judges punish only the deliberate assassin; more, for the parricide is killed but once, while I—for ten weeks I have died day by day, and now I am dying minute by minute. It is too long an agony. Cruel child, why did you love me after having hated me? What mystery fulfills itself in you each week?

Why this crescendo of displeasure, disgust, aversion, fury, cold and contemptuous raillery, and then, suddenly, these tears, this sweetness? Torment of my life! Disastrous love! I would give every experience I have lived through for one day of your ineffable love. But never more, never more! It is too terrible. I cannot believe it, I am going away. I am going—no! However much I suffer, I must not go away. Sainte-Beuve insists that I must stay.

Finally, you loved me again at Venice. Was that my crime? It was my despair. Could I explain [that after you broke with me I had given myself to another]? If I had done so, you would not have allowed me to nurse you, you would have died of rage in submitting to my care. And without me what could you have done, poor dying dove? I have never been able to contemplate what you suffered from your illness, and on my account, without suffering with you. You say that I deceived you. There I was between two men, one of whom was saying, "Return to me, I will repair the wrong I have done you, I will love you, I shall die without you." Meanwhile the other whispered, "Listen to me; you are mine; you cannot forsake me now. Lie. God wills it, God will absolve you."

Ah, poor woman, poor woman, it was then she should have died!

III[1]

. . . but this miserable masculine vanity! From the moment I began to confess, how you treated me! You wanted to strike me, you threatened to proclaim to the world that I was a c——. Yet if I had not lied to you at that time [in Venice] your insane rage would have killed you. And a few days later, if I had not kept on lying, you would have died of grief. Do you think one enjoys lying? There is no greater agony for the guilty. It is their hell on earth.

Then, too, do you realize how horrible it is to lose the respect of one who has loved you, and whom you yourself still love? See how differently I treated *the other!* When he went away, did I make any effort to keep his respect? Did I lie to him? Did I bother to pretend? Did I do anything to prevent him from becoming my enemy? And has he not done me all the harm he could?

. . . full of you. I almost wish you would be cruel to me again to-morrow, because then the day after you would certainly be kind. That is the way you are, my poor reed, struggling between anger and goodness, wounding, then healing me, accusing me unjustly, then taking it back because you cannot help recognizing the truth. You are gentle as a lamb, with the temper of a lion. But so many people come between us that you are not allowed to stop brooding over the "injury" I have done you. Nor can you uproot from your heart the compassion you feel.

Poor Alfred, if no one knew, you would forgive me! But there beside you stands M. Tattet. If you came back to me he would

[1] This copy of the journal is incomplete, as one page is partially destroyed. The beginning of this section, together with what was written on the opposite side of the paper, is therefore missing.—*Aurore Sand.*

say, in that stupid way of his, "Good Lord, what weakness!" Tattet, who falls in the lap of Mademoiselle Déjazet and weeps there when he is drunk! And there are others. You listen to this one and that one. You are told how they gossip about us in a certain esthetic salon. And if you returned to me you know how those ladies would exclaim, "How terribly pathetic! How dreadfully ridiculous!" So you prefer to remain mad and miserable. Besides, what need is there to pardon when you are sure of being loved?

[George Sand was incapable of opposing the least resistance to an illusion. As soon as she let go her imagination, it gathered momentum and became a strong current. Then, as a rising stream carries with it the dry leaves and broken branches on its borders, her imagination grasped at images and metaphors, seizing whatever was nearest, using symbols that had been discarded and outworn. Thus in her journal to Alfred she who had outgrown theology reverted to the religious symbols which had been impressed upon her mind in the convent. Under the influence of strong emotion her memory resuscitated a previous emotional experience. The sometimes exaggerated, sometimes chaotic imagery linked her present obsession to the religious mysticism she had felt at sixteen. In the exaltation of her feeling nothing seemed inappropriate. Bible parables and phrases were summoned to bear witness to her state of suffering. Herself and the Magdalen, Alfred and Jesus, were identified in her consciousness, as the emotion of the present was fused with the emotion of the past. This was the distracted effort of a grief-ridden mind to express in words what can only be expressed in sobs and groans. Her moods change swiftly. Under the pressure of suffering she ascends from emotion to imagery, then, as the pressure is lessened, she descends to commonplace narratives of her daily life, only to be exalted once more by the suffering which again requires imaginative expression for release.

During the period of her hopeless love George Sand's mind was in a state of arrested development. Her powerful personality was in total eclipse. This is especially interesting, as she was described by so many of her contemporaries as the typical strong-minded woman. Many considered her the strongest-minded woman of her times. Yet the caprices of a spoiled boy reduced her to the plight of a female Samson, shorn of her locks and of her strength.]

When you left Venice, if I had realized that you were to feel real love for me and that you were to suffer as I suffer to-day, I would have been willing to cut off the hand that offended you, and I would have said to you, "Throw it into the sea and let the blood flowing from it wash the other clean. Then take my good hand and lead me to the end of the world." If you could accept my atonement I could still atone. Can you?

But to whom is all this raving addressed? To you, walls of my room, echoing my sobs! To you, grave and silent portrait! To you, terrifying skull, full of poison surer than any that kills the body! Or is it to thee, deaf and dumb Christ? In vain for me to talk, in vain to weep and pity myself, thou alone wilt pardon me. Let thy mercy give oblivion to this grief-stricken heart.

Ah, give me back my lover, and I shall be devout! My knees will wear out the pavements of the churches.

Thursday morning.

What is this nonsense that Buloz told me yesterday about M. Liszt? Can Alfred have talked to him? Has Alfred honestly believed for one instant that I was going to fall in love with M. Liszt? Does he still believe it? Ah, my dear, if you could be jealous of me, with what pleasure I would send all those people away! But you are not jealous. You have pretended to believe something you did not believe, in order to rid yourself of me more quickly. That is cruel, and if I could have loved M. Liszt I should have done so in anger at your cruelty. But I could not. What do you make of that, M. Tattet? Now is the time to use your boasted logic.

Here is some logic I heard the other day. I'm glad I don't care for spinach, for if I liked it I should eat it, and I cannot bear spinach.

Again speaking of logic, at Nohant not long ago I was drinking wine with my friend the Gaul [Alphonse Fleury] when he broke out into wild talk about assassinating Louis Philippe. I said, "You sound dangerous. If I did not know how good you are I should consider you wicked, and if I didn't love you I should hate you."

That's what it is to use logic. Be logical, you who can. As for me, I suffer and weep. If I could do anything else I would neither weep nor suffer.

Tell me, what do you consider the surest way of keeping a woman faithful? Can you hold her by moral precepts? Ah, no, my dear, no hearts are safe unless they are guarded by love. But, it is argued—this is the way all husbands argue—if we had to rely on love alone we could never keep our wives faithful. True enough, my lover, there is no way of holding a woman, once you have lost her love.

Buloz advises me to show Liszt to the door. Why should I? For whose sake? Once or twice when we were together I almost thought he was falling in love with me, or that he was ready to do so. If I could have responded, I might perhaps have encouraged him. But under the circumstances I was on the point of telling him—I mean, of making him understand—that it was unthinkable. Then suddenly, during his third visit to my house, I saw clearly that I had been stupidly cherishing an unnecessary virtue. Liszt loves no one but God and the Holy Virgin, who does not resemble me in the slightest degree.

Excellent young man! If his piety is sincere I respect him. If it is an affectation I shall never know the difference. And in either case, why should I send him away? How would I manage it and what reason could I give?

Besides, it is all so unimportant. Nothing has reality for me but one fixed idea, one last hope. That hope is modest indeed for you, poor George—you who were so ambitious to be loved and who are now so humble.

Before me hangs the picture of Magdalen. She weeps and I weep with her. How magnificent her hair is! I am Magdalen shorn of her tresses but carrying her cross and her death's-head. That head at which you looked so sadly, poor sinner, did not teach so terrible a lesson as the skull on my table. You loved Jesus, who said, "Her sins are forgiven, for she loved much."

I also love, but I am not forgiven. How gladly I would exchange my comfortable room and warm dressing-gown for your wilderness and rags if I were permitted to carry with me the words of hope spoken by your Christ as he smiled forgiveness. Mine does not even say, "Let the woman draw near, let her wash my feet."

As I was telling you, Buloz, I have a fixed idea. I want to win back Alfred's friendship and respect. It will take time; six months at least, perhaps more. I am willing to let it take a lifetime. It is the one hope that sustains me, the one idea that has succeeded in getting into this poor head. That is why I cannot decide to leave, for when I am far away—as he himself said—he will imagine I am doing the reckless things he always suspects. It is only just to myself to stay on here where he can observe and judge me. So you see I do not want to isolate myself or live in seclusion. That would seem to him romanticism or madness. He would doubt whether I could live alone like that. At the first step I took outside, he would imagine me as tempted and he would conclude that I had succumbed. Besides, who knows that it might not prove true? Claustration, asceticism, mortification, exalt the senses. Why should I exalt mine by dangerous solitude—I who am unconscious of the senses while living, as I do, in the midst of men?

Not but that I would be willing to live like a nun if he would show me a little affection and come to see me every day. But he would not come, or if he did, it would be in the usual contemptuous mood which is the reaction from his mood of love.

No, I must put behind me a period of time together with some data which may be referred to as a past. I must exhibit a past which will prove to him that I can love, suffer and submit.

My plan is to surround myself with men as high-minded as they are distinguished. I shall not choose powerful men, I prefer to associate with artists: Liszt, Delacroix, Berlioz, Meyerbeer. I hardly know, whom else to choose. I shall be with them as a man among men.

Of course people will gossip. They will deny the possibility of such comradeship. They will laugh at me. Alfred will hear these innuendoes and will get a wrong impression. He will cut himself off from me. Then he will take a mistress, if he has not already done so. But the truth will triumph—O my God, who knows that better than I! A lie will out. But, by the same principle, good deeds are equally convincing. These men who surround me will defend me. They will justify my conduct. Of course they will, unless they are brutes and cads. And if they are, they will be known as such and no one will believe any false statements that they make. I see that I must choose wisely and examine into their characters.

As soon as I can make some more money I shall start housekeeping again and eat at home. Then every evening I shall give a small dinner to two or three friends, as I used to do. I shall work hard. I shall go out more. I must distract myself, strengthen myself against despair.

After I have led this sane and honest life long enough to prove that I can maintain it, I shall go, O my love, to ask you to shake my hand. I shall not torment you with jealousies and persecutions. I realize that when one no longer loves, one no longer loves. But I must have your friendship. I need it in order to endure the love in my own heart and prevent it from killing me.

Oh, if I only had your friendship to-day! I am in such a hurry to win it! What a world of good it will do me! If I had a few lines from you from time to time, one word, permission sometimes to send you one of those little images bought on the quai for four sous, or cigarettes that I roll myself, or a bird, a plaything, anything to cheat my grief and loneliness. Yes, anything to make me imagine that you will think of me a moment while receiving these foolish gifts.

No, it is not calculation, nor prudence, nor fear of what people say. Great heavens, it isn't that! I tell my story to all the world. Everyone knows it, everyone talks of it, everyone laughs at me. But that is unimportant. Ridicule is a small annoyance compared to my immense grief. Let my enemies enjoy themselves; I suffer; I scarcely ever think of them, and when I do it is to pity them for taking their pleasure in such strange ways.

Truly I do not ask you to call on me merely to prove to the world that I am not an unfortunate woman who has been cast off. You did offer, the last time I saw you, to do just that. Did I accept it, tell me? For once do me justice.

But you do not hear me. You are sleeping now, for it is eleven o'clock in the morning.

Yes, I should like to have your friendship. But you do not allow me to try to make you believe in my good intentions. If I should go to you now to make this request there would be stormy scenes, endless scenes, and they would make you ill. As for me— my God, I'd rather have blows than nothing. Nothing—that is the most frightful thing in the world. It is my expiation, let no other be demanded. Sackcloth and ashes, fasting, lashes of the whip, are the only punishments that penitents have known how to devise. They have not conceived the torture inflicted on me. I live three paces from the man I love. I am not allowed to see him. I am forced to control myself, keep calm, laugh, eat!

Then there is jealousy. I shall need time before I can acquire the courage not to be jealous. O my God, you subject me to suffering of which I had not dreamed. But my misery shall be pushed down into the deepest depths of my heart. Not long ago I dined with him [Alfred] at Pinson's, and I was made to realize how vile, unjust and foolish one becomes under the influence of jealousy. He spoke so admiringly of a certain woman that I would willingly have done her harm. That is as ugly as it is stupid.

No, no, Lord God, do not let me become inhuman and soulless!

The capacity for passion is both cruel and divine. The sufferings of love should ennoble, not degrade. Pride is of some use here. Come, my pride, prove your worth and dignity.

May that woman aid him and console him, may she teach him to believe in love. I, alas, have only taught him to deny love. Mea culpa! Alfred, I am going to write a book. You will see that my soul is not vindictive, for this book will be a terrific accusation against myself. Saints in heaven—you have sinned, and how you have suffered!

IV

THE hour of my death draws near. Each day, as it passes, sounds a knell, and in four days the last knell of death will tremble through the life-giving air around me. A tomb will open, and into it my youth and passion will vanish forevermore. What shall I become then? Mournful shade, on the bank of what stream will you wander? Through what immense region of eternal cold?

It takes more courage to commit emotional suicide and live on in the deadness of despair than to drink poison. Oh, my children, you will never know how much I love you.

I had resigned myself to this death in life. God, why did you waken me? Why did you disturb me by sending this vision with the face of a lovely blond child? Phantom of my burning nights, angel of death, fatal love, my destiny! How I still love you, assassin! Let your kisses burn me! Let me be utterly consumed by you! Then throw my ashes to the winds of heaven. They will enrich the flowers which give you pleasure.

What is this fire that devours my heart? It is as though a volcano raged within me. O God, take pity on thy poor creature! Why do others die? Why is it that I cannot succumb under the burden of my sorrows? They say that grief exhausts itself, and that the wounded heart grows insensitive. When will this heart of mine stop rending me? When will it wither and let me know peace?

Never again, blue eyes, will you gaze at me. Lovely head, never again shall I see you press against me, veiled in sweet languor. Warm, supple body, never again will you hover over me, as did Elisha over the dead child, to bring it back to life. No more will you touch my hand as Jesus touched the hand of Jairus' daughter, saying, "Little child, arise." Adieu, golden hair, adieu, white shoulders; adieu to all that once was mine. Henceforth in my ardent nights I shall be driven to embrace the trunks of pine trees or rocks in the forest, crying aloud your name, and when I have dreamed my ecstasy I shall fall fainting on the moist earth.

Why this fixed image in my brain? After all the revolts of reason, all the counsels of truth, all the struggles of a wounded ego, why does thy divine profile come between me and the walls of my room?

Why are the faces of those who talk to me suddenly enveloped in a cloud, while I see on the shoulders of every man the head of the man I adore? Why must I repress within my breast my cries of joy or terror? What are these dreams that whirl about my bed in delirium? Is there a demon in the being I love—a demon who will ride me and torture me as long as love lasts?

What fever sent by celestial vengeance burns in the marrow of my bones? What wrong have I done to be punished by this leonine love I feel within me? Why has my blood changed to fire, and why at the moment of death do I know more flaming embraces than those of men? What fury excites you against me that you should pull me toward my coffin, while you devour my flesh and drink my blood?

Do you want me to kill myself? You say you forbid it. What shall I become if this flame continues to consume me? If I cannot pass one night without crying aloud for you, what shall I do when I have lost you forever? Shall I grow pale like a nun devoured by desire? Shall I go mad and wake the people in these houses with my screams? Yes, you want me to kill myself.

Well, why shouldn't I? The grief I feel at the thought of deserting my children breaks my heart and should absolve me before God for the wrong I may do. My daughter, will she suffer because of my death? Very little. My son . . . Poor child, thou wilt weep bitter tears and thy soul will be wounded forever. When they say to him, "Your mother is dead," oh, those tears, those sobs of my little one! Why agonize over them? I shall no

longer see them, I shall cease to know about the tears of my son.
But now, beforehand, they fall on my heart; already I feel them,
my child's hot tears; it is as if they were rolling down my face.
Poor little fellow! I remember the sorrows of my own childhood;
they were no less intense than those of to-day. And when a
stranger tells thee gently that thy mother is no more, thou wilt
return alone, through those long cold corridors. No, I shall not
kill myself, unless delirium deprives me of reason, as has almost
happened so many times when I have been just on the border.
But the angel of Abraham held out his sword to save my child.
Watch over me, then, God of the orphans. Banish these frightful
temptations. Rouse me from these hours of obsession when it
seems to me that my children cease to exist, when I no longer
know anything but my love and my despair, these ferocious hours
when I should like to tear out my heart. The other night I
dreamed that I buried it under some paving stones. Poor heart,
you are going to be buried alive. How you will suffer until the
stone of the sepulchre has annihilated you by its weight. My son,
my son! I want you to read this some day and know how much I
love you. O my tears, tears of my heart, sign this page, and may
his own tears some day find your traces near his name.

Saturday.

This morning I met Jules Sandeau at Gustave Papet's. He
approached me without embarrassment, and his manner showed
affection and respect. We entered into explanations at once. To
get him to confess, I confessed first. I began by referring to the
unkind remarks about me attributed to him. I confessed that just
at first I had felt hurt and irritated, and I had vented my anger to
certain close friends, notably Papet, who would never repeat
what I said. I added that I was willing to believe his comments
had been exaggerated, but that probably some of them were true.
I did not explain where the reports came from. They were, unfortunately, too convincing. He refused to admit anything and

obstinately denied ever having said one word against me. His insistence was emphatic and none too sincere. Finally he denied ever having made common cause with Planche, or Fremy, Pyat, etc., against me. He does not see them. He is very much hurt by the articles which they write. That is all true. He gave me proof of it, then we talked of other things. I warmed my feet while I smoked a cigarette. Meantime Gustave Papet made his everlasting puns, as usual. Jules, while seeming frank and natural, was really very circumspect. I shook his hand and told him that we must not see each other again because too many people were interested in discussing us, but I asked him not to avoid me when we meet before others but to come and greet me amicably. He asked if he might call on Solange in her boarding school. My permission was cordially given.

I am comforted by this meeting. When two people have loved, it is frightful not to remain friends. For good or ill, they have loved each other. Ah, dear Lord, why does emotion change so, and enter the soul with the same divine fire for a new object! Perhaps in every life there is only one great love. Which has it been in my life? Aurélian? In my heart of hearts it seems the most beautiful. But a love without union is mystic and incomplete. First love is the most ideal—and last love the most real and inescapable. That is what is killing me now.

Then must I die so young? Dear God, save me! If only I could return to religion. If I could adore Jesus as he is adored by nuns!

[After the break with her lover, George, through her devoted friend, Jules Boucoiran, sent Alfred the precious manuscript containing her revelations of the suffering she had endured for his sake. This was a fine gesture of reckless trust, as the midnight ravings of a broken heart are apt to seem ridiculous when read by daylight in the calm aftermath of a passion that has been outlived.

George Sand's motive in confiding her manuscript to Alfred was the hope of softening his memories. A few months earlier she had written to Musset, "If we had parted in a mood of anger, without understanding or explanation, what misery we would have created for ourselves! Bitter memories would have poisoned our lives. Never again would we have been able to believe in anything. But it would be impossible for us to part like that. We have attempted it in vain many times, and each time, as soon as we found ourselves alone, our hearts, however hot with pride and resentment, have almost broken in sorrow and regret. No, that must never happen. In renouncing a bond that has become impossible, we must keep the sense of being related to each other throughout eternity."

When Musset received George's journal the effect on his heart was not so softening as she had hoped. He exhibited the manuscript to others, and indulged in witticisms at the expense of the woman he had so greatly loved. The manner in which he commented on the confession intended for his eyes alone, is described by his brother Paul: [1]

"The man of the world [Alfred] made a grimace as he thought of her appearance in a *bousingot* as she sat in the parterre of the theater. Had there been [in the journal] so much as two words conveying genuine emotion they most assuredly would have touched his heart—but he did not find those words. His memories of the past, his fatal experience, told him that pride was still there, disguised beneath the mask of humility. The last letter astonished him by a force of language which gave every evidence of passion; but 'leonine love' excited his fear more than his interest. . . .

"To rid himself of the melancholy effect of these letters he went to dine with his friend." [Alfred Tattet]

In the text of Paul de Musset's *Lui et Elle* are incorporated eleven printed pages taken from the manuscript of George Sand's journal to Alfred. The book, like all scurrilous sheets, was of course widely read, with the result that the ravings of George's love madness, which she offered to Alfred in the hope of softening his heart, were accepted as her public confession of guilt. Her friends urged her to sue Paul de Musset for libel but she wisely refrained.

[1] *Lui et Elle*, by Paul de Musset, p. 208.

Recklessness and trustfulness were two of George Sand's weaknesses. However, as is usually the case after the madness of love is over, as time went on she had reason to feel less reckless and less trusting, and two years after the conclusion of her love affair she wanted her ravings returned.

The history of her effort to recover the confidential communication, of which the sole copy had been sent to Alfred de Musset, is related by Madame Karénine.[1]

"In 1836 George Sand, through Countess d'Agoult, asked Musset to return her letters. It is not known why the exchange did not take place. In 1840 George Sand again expressed the wish to have her letters sent back. Musset acceded to this request without letting her know that he was forced to demand her journal and certain of her letters from Madame Jaubert, the woman to whom Musset gave the endearing name of 'Godmother' but whose relation to him was in reality a great deal closer.

"Why did Musset place the letters and the journal in the hands of this woman? It is impossible to answer, but it is an established fact that after Musset asked for these documents, Madame Jaubert and her daughter, Countess Legrange, and even Madame Jaubert's maid, spent the entire night making a copy of the journal. In the morning the original was delivered to Musset, who gave it to Gustave Papet, the friend designated by George Sand.

"Madame Jaubert concealed from Musset that a copy remained in her possession. Musset on his part considered it unnecessary to warn George Sand that her journal had been loaned to others. Afterwards, other copies having been made from Madame Jaubert's, one came into the possession of Paul de Musset. Thus the secret was violated and that which had been intimate was made public. But in passing from hand to hand and mouth to mouth, the true story was disfigured by involuntary or premeditated exaggerations, by alterations and fabrications, until finally this sincere narrative, this song of wounded love, commenced to seem to those who had never seen the journal itself and who knew of it only by hearsay, an accusation written by George Sand against herself. Paul de Musset made use of it later on, with a lack of conscience that was wholly exceptional.

[1] *George Sand, sa Vie et ses Œuvres*, Vladimir Karénine. Vol. II, pp. 108-110.

"To show the reader how fully Alfred de Musset realized his brother's lack of good faith, it is sufficient to recall the words which, according to a letter from George Sand to Sainte-Beuve, he [Alfred] addressed to Papet [when Alfred's own letters to George were handed to Papet for the purpose of future publication]: 'There is but one thing I exact of you. I must have your word of honor that you will never give any of these letters to my brother.' After that let readers, biographers and critics continue to have faith in Paul de Musset as the biographer, historian and advocate of his brother."

In the Sand-Musset correspondence there is a letter in which Alfred apparently expressed his frank opinion of his brother Paul. George eliminated these eight lines from Alfred's letter with the following note:

"At this point I have cut out certain criticisms which would have given me a thorough revenge against certain persons. I have destroyed the clipping, as I did not wish to be tempted to punish, even after my death."]

Daily Conversations
With the Very Learned and Highly Skilled
DOCTOR PIFFOËL
Professor of Botany and Psychology
1837

PREFACE

DURING a period that was filled with worry, disruption and overwork, George Sand, here transformed into "Doctor Piffoël," [1] writes about life and people in passing moods of bitterness or enthusiasm.

The following pages disclose her ardent faith and habitual generosity. They also show her occasional explosions of revolt, and her capacity for merciless self-criticism. Sometimes credulous, sometimes skeptical, she reveals or observes herself. In the lamentations which are the complaint of a wounded spirit, one recognizes the fundamental conflicts that explain her life.

"Time and again I have borne on my shoulders heavy yokes of iron. So long as they were placed there with affectionate persuasion and in the name of love and tenderness, I have bowed submissively beneath the beloved hand. But when my friend, grown tired of persuasion, has resorted to commands, when my submission has been claimed, no longer in the name of love and friendship but by reason of some right or power, I have drawn upon the strength that is buried in my nature, I have straightened my shoulders and thrown off the yoke. I alone know the latent force hidden within me. I alone know how much I grieve and suffer and love."

In these words of hers one finds a resurgence of the indomitable force which made the Koenigsmarcks, her ancestors, lords of war and impassioned heroes, and which made their son a Marshal Saxe who could win battles while dying. The bravery of this lineage, its enthusiastic soul, its free intelligence, came to flower in the incomparable woman who was George Sand.

[1] The name Piffoël given to George Sand by herself and by Liszt and Marie d'Agoult was derived from her aquiline nose. [The word *pif* is a colloquial name for nose.] The children of Piffoël called themselves the Piffolini. *Vide* letter from Balzac to George Sand.—*Aurore Sand.*

When she wrote the lines quoted above, George Sand had submitted to many years of suffering before instigating a suit for judicial separation from her husband (1835). At the conclusion of this law suit (August 1836) she went with her children to join Madame d'Agoult and Liszt in Switzerland. She returned to Nohant in October, then went to Paris, and lived at 21 Rue Lafitte in the Hotel de France, where her friends were staying. The affection of these two superior beings who understood and loved her might have brought peace to George's soul had she not been emotionally involved with Everard [Michel of Bourges].

The journal entitled *"Daily conversations with the very learned and highly skilled Dr. Piffoël,"* reveals the mental state of the woman genius at this period. From the spring of 1837 and during the following summer George Sand lived at Nohant, where she entertained several friends, among others, Liszt and Madame d'Agoult. But in the midst of this visit George was forced to leave abruptly for Paris to take care of her dying mother. Directly afterward she went to Fontainebleau to rest for a time, accompanied by her son Maurice, then fourteen years of age. Her rest there was interrupted by a hurried journey to Guillery, where her husband, Casimir Dudevant, had taken their daughter Solange, whom he had kidnaped during George's absence. Legal proceedings followed, but in the winter of 1837-1838 George Sand returns to Nohant, where she devotes herself to her children.

AURORE SAND

FOREWORD BY GEORGE SAND

YES, my dear kind doctor, writing a journal implies that one has ceased to think of the future and has decided to live wholly in the present. It is an announcement to fate that you expect nothing more. It is an assertion that you take each day as it comes and make no connection between to-day and other days. Writing a journal means that facing your ocean you are afraid to swim across it, so you attempt to drink it drop by drop. It means that you count the last leaves of a tree whose trunk has lost its sap.

When you are in the mood to write a journal the passions have cooled, or else they have so far frozen that they may be examined as safely as ice-bound mountains are explored in the season when no avalanches fall. No one should allow himself to solidify to this extent unless he is in a state of such upheaval that all the fires of his being are in danger of eruption. Then indeed it may be necessary to harden the outer crust in order to check the explosion and save the inner flame from becoming extinct.

June 1.

I AWAKENED feeling dull. Piffoël's sleep was disturbed by elusive desires that floated in a pale mist of dreams. The weather is neither cheerful nor depressing. It makes me restless. The trees are tossed by gusty, fantastic wind. The sun is hidden. If I put on my dressing-gown I am too hot, if I take it off I am cold. Leaden day in which I shall accomplish nothing worth while. Tired and apathetic brain! I have been drinking tea in the hope that it would carry this mood to a climax and so put an end to it.

No letter from Everard to-day. He is angry again. Happy man, to find anything worth getting angry about!

Before going to bed.

From midnight until one o'clock I explained to Duteil the theory of dissatisfaction with life. I was indignant because he tried to make me believe he is happy every day and almost every hour of the day. Isn't it exasperating to be treated as a fool by people who do not suffer?

Late at night, June 2.

Piffoël walked twelve miles to-day. As soon as life becomes bearable we stop analyzing it. A tranquil day is spoiled by being examined. Shall we always be guided by feeling which distorts our ideas and impressions? Excessive emotion is like cross-eyed vision whose errors our reason tries feebly to correct.

Noon, June 3.

Magnificent day. Glorious sun, a reign of color. Three linden trees whose feathery tops I see from my bed are the mirror in which I find the weather reflected. Their wide curtain of foliage and a tiny bit of sky are all I can see, but it is enough to tell me what kind of day it is, even before my window is opened. In these trees I see wind effects which are inexplicable. They almost make me believe in the existence of aërial spirits and other freakish beings.

I see, too, how closely the sun rays unite with the green of the leaves, changing their intensity of color as the atmosphere is more or less clear. To-day the light is so alive that a mild wind does not disturb the steady gold of the sun rays and the depth of shadow on the foliage.

You live. No use asking whether life will bring you pleasure or unhappiness, whether it will prove a blessing or a curse. Who could answer these questions? You live, you breathe. The sky is marvelous.

Arabella's [Madame d'Agoult's] room is on the ground floor under mine. Franz's piano is there. My window, before which the lindens are swaying, is just above the window whence come those sounds that the whole world would love to hear. In this place, away from the world, only the nightingales are jealous.

Supreme artist, you are sublime in great things, superior in the little things of life! Nevertheless you are unhappy, consumed by secret conflict. Fortunate man, you are loved by a beautiful woman who is generous, intelligent, chaste. What more do you desire, miserable ingrate? Ah, if only *I* were loved!

If you were loved, Piffoël, you would be ambitious. You are not ambitious because you are not loved.

How wise you are, Piffoël, how profoundly wise! You are a true philosopher. You see your life with such complete understanding. Those wretched baubles which you have not learned to covet are so easily weighed in your firm hand. My compliments, dear Piffoël, I congratulate you.

What a melancholy animal you are!

When Franz plays I am soothed. My griefs are etherealized, my instincts are exalted. He touches the chord of generosity and awakens my response. At times he evokes a note of anger, and it merges with my own. But he never sounds the note of hate. As for me, hatred devours me. Hatred of what? Shall I never find anyone worth hating? Grant me this favor, Lord, and I promise never again to ask for the one worth loving.

Why should the thought of satisfied hate seem fascinating? Because it would be as big as generosity, because it would make one feel magnificent, if only for one hour in a lifetime. One could believe in you then, jealous you who love to hide your greatness from others and exult in it alone.

I love those broken phrases which he flings from the piano and which rest with one foot in the air, dancing off into space like little lame elves. The leaves of the linden steal the melody and complete it with mysterious whispering, as if they were confiding nature's secret to one another.

Perhaps he is composing something, trying it out bit by bit on the piano. At his side are his pipe, his ruled paper and his pens. After he has traced his thought on paper, he confides it to his instrument, whose voice reveals it to listening, receptive nature.

No, I prefer to imagine he is not composing. It seems to me that he walks up and down his room, given over to tumultuous uncertain ideas. Then, in passing the piano, he throws out those whimsical phrases unconsciously. They must be the result of instinctive feeling and not a labor of the brain. Those rapid, impetuous melodies affect me as though I were watching the destruction of a vessel battered by the tempest. I also am torn asunder as I remember what I have suffered while living through a storm at sea.

White Arabella, I was talking of you last night as I walked with Alphonse under brilliant stars in the cool wind that blew at midnight. What is more appealing, I asked, than a strong woman whose pride has been humbled? The white lily whose pliant stem bends at a touch of the wind is more lovable than the yellow lily who refuses to be subdued by the elements.

Piffoël, why the devil can't *you* lower your head when a storm

is upon you? Why are your tears so bitter? Why must you break
without having bent? You turn to your master as the heliotrope
lifts her head to the sun, and of your own free will you like to
acknowledge his glory. But if he hides behind clouds and sends
down storm and thunder, you shrivel and break, for you will not
yield to force.

Piffoël, dear friend, I believe your liver is out of order.

June 4.

While I was at Coudray I fell asleep in the deep grass and slept
there for some time. As I roused myself and lay half awake, with
eyes smarting from the sun's heat and with vision clouded by the
hot vapor which the hay exhales at noontime, I found myself
possessed by an amusing illusion. Lying close to the ground as I
was, the high grass overtopped my face and limited my view to a
narrow bit of space where grass and field flowers were silhouetted
against the transparent blue of the air.

For the moment I lost all sense of dimension, and those tenuous
weeds took on enormous proportions. Their slight bodies seemed
to me transformed into various trees which the grasses resemble
in miniature. One was the tall, slender palm, another the weeping
willow. A blade of ripe oats above my head seemed ready to crush
me by letting fall its gigantic fruit, and in the distance—of a
few feet—I caught the vision of other superb trees. Serried rows
of purple sumac and of spiny aloes, cactus, cedars of Lebanon,
banana trees with their voluptuous, outspread leaves, orange trees
in flower, luxuriant catalpa, robust oaks and pale olive trees took
the place of tiny field flowers, fine aigrettes and delicate filaments,
silky tufts and dangling seed pods in which the meadows abound.
The space between their stems was filled with short grass like a
thick undergrowth. As I looked at those weeds, which a hot
breeze stirred feebly, they seemed to me an immeasurable forest
which bent beneath the force of a powerful storm. Its heavy
branches were shattered by the tempest, and the lofty tree-tops

crashed with a terrifying noise. In the midst of this tumult a dull roaring sound came to my ears. Gripped by terror at the approach of a lion, I leaped to my feet—and it was well that I did, for a big hornet was buzzing under my nose. But alas, the virgin forest and the mighty exotic trees had disappeared. I found myself surrounded by nothing more intimidating than clover, alfalfa, grass and other kinds of fodder.

So that was the end of my solitary journey into the wilds of the New World.

June 5.

Magnificent weather, a great deal of wind with mighty noise. Movements full of grace among the leaves of the lindens. They remind me of the proud and gracious gestures of Arabella.

I awoke feeling stupid. My sleep was calm and deep, but my sore throat hangs on.

Why doesn't that confounded piano wake up! What shall I do with myself this morning?

The Lord be praised, my friend has heard me. Here come the first melodies of the Andante of the Pastoral Symphony of Beethoven.

True summer music.

Among his old unpublished papers Hoffmann [1] left titles for the concluding chapters of *Kreyssler*. There are two which have especially impressed me—"Sound of the North"—"Sound of the South." I am interested in getting at the sense of such a distinction in the poetry of music. I look for it in nature and in his own primitive melodies, which I then combine with known effects in music, and I follow along, trying to find a clear and satisfying understanding of these mysterious designations.

That these titles suggest an inspired idea is obvious, but how the idea should be interpreted is not so plain. In attempting to find

---

[1] Ernst Theodor Amadeus Hoffmann, 1776-1822. German romance writer of eccentric imagination, operatic composer and musical director, portrait and mural painter, counselor-at-law. Celebrated as the author of *Tales of Hoffmann*.

its meaning, one is in danger of getting lost in perceptions that are purely poetic or that are as vague as Hoffmann himself is at times.

But Hoffmann's vagueness is in his style and not in his thought. No man has ever penetrated the world of dreams with greater frankness or with finer observation, nor has anyone used so much logic, sense and reason in the realm of fantasy and poetic reverie. No mind has been less subjugated by imagination. Yet imagination was Hoffmann's vital element, his real world.

If there is anything in phrenology, his dominant characteristic must have been the power to marvel.

In spite of the foolish exaggerations quoted and published about his eccentricities, W. Loève-Veimar's excellent biography (based on revelations contained in intimate letters and journals) proves that his mind was entirely sound. Additional proof is found in Hoffmann's writings and in the records of his life.

A sensitive organization and a singular diversity of gifts made him a writer of the first order. He must not be regarded as a miserable artist tormented by insatiable desires for success. His powers were so remarkable and varied that he literally did not know what to do with them. Inevitably, therefore, the world of fantasy appealed to him because of its apparently limitless scope.

Hardly had he entered the field of literature before he realized the limitations of its straight and narrow paths. He continued to walk in them, maintaining the poise of a mind preëminently logical. This detachment, which he preserves in the midst of his visions, explains the great charm of his whimsical creations. In them one always senses (to use the ingenious metaphysical language of Sporzheim) the man of causality and eventuality governing and directing the man who is inspired to marvel and idealize.

If sometimes his method of expression seems vague, it is due to the undeveloped state of language, for even the most beautiful of human languages is still in the barbaric stage. The words which are needed to express intuitions of an exalted order do not yet exist.

What Hoffmann feels never comes to expression in anything resembling delirium. It stands the test of reason. Beyond his smiling phantoms and behind his symbolic abstractions is profound thought, together with an effort toward a science of the soul. Nothing he wrote was conceived by chance. He created supernatural beings by exaggerating the reality of human beings whom he knew so well how to observe. The devil appears in his imagery only as a philosophical principle. In studying his work more attentively than the average mind considers worth while, one finds in each naïve reality and in every material observation some trace of the principle that animates his poetic imaginings. This is equally true of the musical compositions of the great masters. They all have been inspired by feeling. They all contain an intuitive sense that can be translated into thought.

Certain critics who pretend or believe that they are specialists in knowledge, ridicule the theory of a moral and intellectual interpretation of harmonic combinations, and attribute the overpowering effect of these combinations to purely imaginary connections between sounds and mental images. But some of these connections are so real, so palpable, that it is by no means impossible for the artist's ear to apprehend them. Hoffmann, more explicit, richer in power of expression than most artists, could even translate them into popular language which the public understands. He thus made a great step forward. In painting and in music he popularized the exquisite in poetic perception.

June 6.

Superb weather. Hideous sore throat and black melancholy for thirty-six hours.

After the desolation of winter, when spring is bringing new life, man, of all animate beings, wearies most quickly and most completely of the delights of outside nature. He attributes his inner perturbations to changes in the atmosphere, and so excuses the unevenness of his moods, the susceptibility of his miserable nerves. But when the sun is shining in a sapphire sky, when a happy wind is singing among the leaves and softly rocking the branches, when the whole world is intoxicated with perfume, fresh air, light, and love, why does this shabby creature still continue his disconsolate wail? Why is his capacity for happiness so short-lived that it cannot last through one week of pleasant weather?

[The following extracts from the Piffoël journal bear directly upon Michel of Bourges.

Michel was the republican leader of his province. He was called the great man of Berry. When, in her legal proceedings against her husband, Michel became her lawyer, George fell under the spell of his dominant mind and bowed to his authority. During the period of Michel's political activities she nursed him in sickness, cared for him in prison, and neglected her work to build up his career. Now, at the height of his power and reputation, he was so occupied with the needs of his ego that he had no consideration or sympathy for her.

George loved Michel the more because he had been a peasant. She liked to rise above class distinctions and recognize greatness of soul. But Michel's greatness lay in energy, egotism, and ambition. His soul remained commonplace. Nor was his mind as remarkable as George supposed. His sympathies were limited by his own experiences. He had always seen women toiling in the fields, obedient to their masters, and since fate had made him one of their masters, he was content to let the arrangement stand. The fact that George was a superior woman had at first commanded his admiration, but after they became lovers, the very superiority which had attracted him aroused his anger and hurt his vanity.

Like many another self-made man, Michel was the victim of what we call to-day an inferiority complex. George, of course, did not recognize his neurosis. She only knew that his vanity was immoderate and that his thirst for adulation seemed unquenchable.

Michel was in the habit of summoning George to meet him, at his own convenience, when business called him to one of the neighboring towns, La Châtre or Châteauroux. At the present writing, George is about to obey one of these summons. She has been wounded by Michel's unfaithfulness and neglect. Her feeling for him has changed. But she is still sufficiently in love to gallop on horseback to Châteauroux at his demand. She prepares for departure in a mood of discouragement.]

June 6.

I must leave to-morrow. Deceitful fate, where are your promises of hope? You do not dare tempt me any more, you do not dare encourage me as you used to do, saying, Go and you will be happy. You are silent, for you know that I have found you out. I despise you. Wherever I go, I shall go without faith in you. I shall go alone. Despondent about myself, relentless toward myself—because of myself.

[She returns home in a mood of strong reaction. Her soul is rested at the sight of familiar surroundings. Every least thing about her own room becomes dear to her. She knows herself deceived. She feels old. She has temporarily attained a mental attitude of detachment which she regards as a high peak of spiritual achievement. She knows she is unable to maintain this height. Impersonal detachment appears and disappears throughout this period of George Sand's life. It is not until she is forty-two that she succeeds in making it a fairly permanent habit of mind.]

In my room at sunrise, June 11.

Friendly walls, welcome me home again. Your white and blue paper gladdens my eyes. How happy the birds are, singing in the garden! The spray of honeysuckle in my glass is sweet.

Piffoël, Piffoël, what fearful calm is this in thy soul? Does it mean that the flame has burned out?

I salute you, wonderful Piffoël! Wisdom abides with you. Suffering has taught you at last that you are the greatest dupe on earth.

Blessed weariness, mother of repose, descend upon us poor dreamers now and at the hour of our death. So be it.

Consider, Piffoël. Here you are on one of the peaks of the mountain. You can wing your way toward the clouds, or walk the humdrum paths that lead down to the valley. Which do you choose—well-worn paths, or a strong flight? Beauty awaits you if you can reach the heights.

Alas, when the raven is old his wing feathers begin to fall. Turn your gaze toward the valley. For heaven is closed to you. It has nothing more to teach you save the secrets of death.

[Two days after her journey to Châteauroux, George confides to Piffoël her suppressed feelings about this painful visit, and heaps imprecations upon her lover's head.

It is interesting to observe that George Sand turned a different side of her being toward each man she loved. Michel's George bore little resemblance to the woman who once adored the poet Musset. Toward Musset she had been self-abnegating almost to self-annihilation. For him she had sacrificed pride and self-respect. When the poet was cruel she had become gentle and submissive. But the tyranny of Michel aroused an amount of anger and bitterness which one might have concluded, from her softness toward Musset, did not exist in her nature.

This seeming inconsistency is explained by George Sand herself. "When my friend has resorted to commands, when my submission has been claimed by reason of some right or power, I have drawn upon the latent strength hidden in my nature. I have straightened my shoulders and thrown off the yoke."

Musset, in moods of contrition, had begged and entreated her love, while Michel, less fine and sensitive, demanded it as a right.

In the following pages George asks Dr. Piffoël how far a woman should go in proving her devotion to a man.]

Brilliant sun. Sparkling, immobile lindens. June 13.
Should she devote herself to him in all ways at all times, cheerfully, enthusiastically, with religious fervor? Must she never consider herself? Must she expose herself to the vulgar jokes of the

public, to its hatred and unjust contempt? Must she risk the loss of family and friends, accepting in their place poverty, weariness, and persecution? Is she to sacrifice her art and cut herself off from the life of ideas? Is she called upon to accept his faults and vices? Must she veil them in mystery so she will never see them and judge them? Is she expected to do more than this, and even love his vices and make them her own, although they seem to her revolting?

At night while she is sitting by the fire, warm, or even drenched in perspiration, shall she, in answer to his summons, rush forth into the freezing cold, in order to satisfy his whims or spare him a momentary disappointment?

Must she be as blind, attentive, and indefatigable toward her lover as a tender mother is to her first-born?

No, Piffoël, there is no need of such excessive devotion. Besides, it counts for nothing unless it is combined with adulation.

You have sometimes imagined, Piffoël, that a woman might say to the object of her love, "You are a human being like me. I chose you out of all the world because I believed you the greatest and best of men. But now, since you often make me suffer, I no longer know what you are. It seems to me that, like other men, you have imperfections. Besides, there is no perfection in man or woman. But I don't mind your faults. I don't mind my sufferings. In fact, I prefer your faults to the virtues of any other man. I accept you. I have you, and you have me also, for I withhold nothing of myself, my life, my thoughts, my actions, my beliefs —I submit them all to you. I subordinate everything to your happiness, for I chose you with the idea that you were to be my all. This idea so controls me that my thoughts are no longer my own. You may misguide me, lose me, lead me to death and infamy—for me the world outside of you has ceased to exist. Morality, philosophy, are words without meaning. There is no logic but your instinct, no truth but my love. I have no future and no destiny except in your future and your destiny. Happiness, unhappiness, what difference do they make! I accept the wounds, and would willingly submit to the tortures, of human experience. I shall glory in any humiliation if I may soften for you the harshness of life and rest your heart on mine."

No, no, Piffoël, Doctor of Psychology, you are nothing but a fool. That is not the language a man wants to hear. He accepts devotion as a matter of course. He regards it as his by inherent right, for the simple reason that he came forth from the body of Madame his mother. He attributes to himself a power of intelligence and will which makes any independence on the part of his friend unbearable. He scorns her in proportion to the goodness, sacrifice, abnegation and mercy which he finds in her. Domination, possession, absorption, are but the conditions on which he consents to allow her to adore him as a god. He does not realize that whoever is adored as a god is deceived, mocked, and fawned upon.

Man knows himself necessary to woman.

He has therefore acquired an almost fatuous self-confidence. And the majority of women, whether from cupidity, or sex need, or vanity, have so much at stake in their love for men that they allow men to arrogate to themselves a despotic power over their lives.

When for any one of these reasons her tyrant becomes indispensable, woman faces the double problem of holding her tyrant and lightening her yoke. There is but one means of achieving these two ends, and that is by the basest sort of flattery. Submission, loyalty, tender care and devotion a man takes for granted. He ceases to value them because they are given him for nothing. Unless he receives all these from a woman, he will not deign to bother with her at all.

She must do more for him. She must prostrate herself before him and say to him, "You are great, sublime, incomparable. You are more perfect than God. Your face radiates light, where your feet have trod nectar is distilled, you have nothing remotely resembling a fault, and you have all conceivable virtues. No living soul is your equal—I speak not merely for myself, dazzled as my eyes are by the splendor of your glance, but for the whole stupid mass of inferior people, who by rights should fall on their knees as you pass by and proclaim you king of the universe. When you strike me I am glorified, when you push me aside with your foot my fate is preferable to that of all other beings. Belonging to you is such a privilege that every member of the human race envies me. As I look about me I see no one who is not dying for the honor of being in my place."

In ecstatic moods it must be admitted that aberrations like these may be sincere. They do sometimes come to expression. But if they are not followed now and then by violent reactions, do not believe in them, imbecile, for she who adores you continuously without intervals of criticism, despises you in secret, and only the woman who accepts you as imperfect, and endures you though unjust, gives you proof of disinterested love. But, vain creature, you do not want a woman who knows how to forgive, you want a woman who pretends to believe that you have never done anything that needs forgiveness. You want her to caress the hand that strikes her and kiss the mouth that lies to her.

Very good, since you insist on being an idol of clay, seek the object of your love in the mire, and see to it that you stifle her every desire to emerge from her ignominious condition. For if woman lifts herself up, you would be forced, in order to remain her superior, to lift yourself also. And to purify yourself—and that is what you cannot and will not do.

Therefore, my dear Piffoël, apply yourself to study the science of life, and when next you set about writing a novel, try to show more understanding of the human heart. Never choose for your ideal a woman who is strong, disinterested, courageous and candid. The public will hiss her and greet her with the odious name of Lélia, whom they call incapable.

Incapable, yes. Thank heaven! Incapable of servility, sycophancy, baseness, incapable of being afraid of you. You, stupid one, who believe in laws which punish murder by murder, you who have no power of vengeance except in calumny and defamation! When you find a woman who knows how to live without you, your vain power turns to fury.

Your fury shall be punished by a smile, by an adieu, and by life-long unconcern!

[This eruption from George Sand's inner volcano, ending as it does on the note of finality, might seem to indicate that all was over between her and her lover. But she did not break with him until the following September.

George Sand has often been accused of heartlessness because she seemed to recover so quickly from disappointment in love. The truth was that instead of struggling against an irrational passion, it was her habit to let it exhaust itself completely before she broke its bonds. The last stages of a love affair were therefore her period of convalescence. By the time the break occurred her heart was healed. And since, during all the agonies of delayed separation, she had mourned her love as dead, her period of mourning was over when her friends expected it to begin.

If George had really bidden Michel farewell, as she felt moved to do, at the time of this writing, his hold on her imagination would have enabled him to win her back again. For although she was angered by his tyrannies and hurt by his neglect, she still cared for him, as the violence of her feeling conclusively proves. In June, therefore, we may assume that her recovery was slowly taking place but was by no means completed.

During the summer George Sand's miserable state of mind was somewhat ameliorated by the visit to Nohant of Franz Liszt and Madame d'Agoult. She had been with them in Switzerland the previous summer, and in Paris the early part of the past winter. During all these months the three-cornered friendship between the two unusual women and the great musician seemed as perfect as it was picturesque.

No man among all her friends was so akin to George Sand as Franz Liszt. Their histories present a series of striking similarities. Both Sand and Liszt were mystics. They longed for spiritual union with something greater than self. During adolescence both were exalted by ascetic idealism; Liszt longed to become a priest, Sand wanted to be a nun. Again, at about the same age—he at nineteen and she at seventeen—each was possessed by an intellectual fever of reading. They even chose and preferred the same books. First love with Liszt was a spiritual passion for Caroline de Saint-Cricq. George Sand's first love was a mystic union with Aurélien de Sèze. In youth both Sand and Liszt adored Victor Hugo and embraced the cult of romanticism. Later on they sympathized with Saint-Simonism, shared identical democratic ideas, and admired the Christian Socialist Lamennais. In maturity both repudiated the doctrine of art for art's sake, and merged convictions and ideals with art.

These two natures, driven by the creative urge, finding only transient satisfaction and always seeking ultimate peace, were deeply rooted in religion. But as they approached old age their religious needs grew more and more dissimilar. The mind of Liszt accepted without question the tenets of the Catholic Church, whereas George's intellectual development left all theology far behind. George found ultimate peace in impersonal love for humanity and nature, while Liszt joined the Franciscan order, became an abbé and wore a cassock. In the celibacy of old age he blamed George for his youthful follies. (They all blamed George when they grew old, as grown-up children trace their faults to an indulgent mother.) But in their years of close association Liszt proved his friendship by numerous letters that breathed affection and admiration. He also wrote to George his *Bachelor of Music*, and planned to set *Consuelo* to music, although for lack of opportunity the opera was never composed.

George could not have fallen in love with Liszt, because he was neither sick like Chopin, nor naughty like Musset, nor in need of sustenance for his ego, like Michel of Bourges. In character as well as temperament Liszt was, like George, endowed with strength. George selected her lovers with no assistance from her intellect. Her attractions were instinctive and self-destructive. Liszt's fancies were equally irrational. He could never have thought of self-reliant George as an object of passion. His ideal woman was a golden-haired angel disguised on earth as a princess. Marie d'Agoult had marvelous yellow hair and the proud bearing which fairy tales ascribe to royalty. So of course the dreamy music master fell in love with her. But unfortunately the reckless Countess abandoned her husband, her two children, and her social position to follow Liszt to Switzerland, and in the cramped quarters of a commonplace hotel his dream was spoiled. He found that princesses are brought up to be worldly and extravagant, and that angels who descend to earth acquire tiresome affectations and poses.

Liszt, as George Sand observed, was the victim of many conflicts. In his inner life the ambition of a successful virtuoso vied with the creative urge of a great composer. His mind was divided, also, between an ascetic ideal and the worship of heaven-sent women, while his heart was torn between the desire for freedom and the need of love. "A loving woman," he said, "is a man's guardian angel." But when his Countess clung to him with the desperation always noticeable in those who have given all for love, he found he could not compose music with a woman's arms around his neck.

As soon as the lovers emerged from their voluntary exile in Switzerland, it seemed as though the Countess had sacrificed her life in vain. She became an inconvenience. When Liszt went into society she was ostracized; when he went on concert tours she was a nuisance. In creative moods he wanted to dream in solitude, but there beside him stood his loving woman, anxious and willing to be the inspiration of his dreams. He endured hearing her call herself his Beatrice, until in a mood of resentment he lost self-control and told her, "Real Beatrices die at eighteen." This was rather bitter, as Madame d'Agoult was twenty-eight at the time of their elopement. Whenever Liszt cut loose from her he rebelled against domestic ties by indulging in hectic love affairs, as George Sand had reacted from the long suppression of unhappy marriage.

In the summer of 1837 Marie d'Agoult had not yet won distinction. Her ambition was beginning to awake. Having burned all her bridges behind her, she determined to compensate for the loss of her salon by making a name for herself in literature. With this purpose in mind she emulated George Sand, choosing a man's name as her friend had done and calling herself Daniel Stern. Having studied and admired *Lélia,* she wrote the novel *Nélida.*

Liszt was unkind enough to say, "If there had been no *Lélia* there would have been no *Nélida*."

George turned her masculine side to Liszt. She felt completely at home with him. They liked each other calmly, as men do. In the evening, after the others had retired, the two friends sat at opposite ends of the long dining-room table, George writing her novel, Franz working on the script of some music.

There was none of this silent companionship between the two women. George treated Marie as a courtier might, admiring her beauty, praising her talents, and encouraging her efforts to write. She invented sentimental names for her and called her "white Arabella" or "the Princess." She also played the pedagogue, as toward a pupil, teaching the self-engrossed Countess the love of nature and astronomy. But Arabella was never truly interested in the stars, and although she liked the bunch of violets George placed in her room every day, she could not share George's enthusiasm for the study of plants and bugs.

Marie d'Agoult's character was full of inconsistencies. When she ran away with Liszt she surrendered her children but clung tenaciously to her husband's title. Liszt offered her his name but she refused it with scorn. George Sand reversed these values. When she separated from her husband she surrendered his title but clung tenaciously to her children. Indeed, democratic George and the aristocratic Countess differed in many essentials. Madame Karénine sums up the contrast of the two women's characters:

"George Sand, the personification of straightforwardness, did everything, whether good or bad, with uncovered face, while the Countess was always veiled. The affectations of the Countess drove George Sand outside of herself and led her to cynicism. The cynicism of George Sand influenced the Countess to hypocrisy.

"Insensibly dissonances arose between the great novelist, already celebrated, and the Countess who had no other title to glory than that of being the mistress of a great virtuoso. It has often been remarked that the glory of George Sand troubled the Countess's sleep.

"But even apart from jealousy, harmony could not long exist between a nature nakedly revealed and one artificially concealed."

At the time of their visit to Nohant, Liszt and Marie were still in love, and the relation of the three friends was harmonious, while George's feeling for Marie was in the stage of uncritical enthusiasm. The following effusion written about Madame d'Agoult is an example of George Sand's most admired romantic style.

One easily pictures the scene of that summer evening at Nohant. George Sand sits on the steps that lead from the French window to the garden. She is in the midst of her family group. They talk and laugh and tease her for remaining silent. But in her silence her imagination is stirred by the sound of Liszt's music. She projects her own response into the plants and flowers, the trees and moon and listening nightingale. In an hour or so she will retire to her room to write on her novel. But her imagination will not easily change its center. The picture it creates is so vivid that as soon as she is alone she will hastily jot it down in her journal before she begins her night's work.]

June 12.

This evening, while Franz was playing fantastic melodies of Schubert, the Princess walked in the shadows that fall across the terrace. She was wearing a dress of indefinite color. Her head and tall, slender body were swathed in a long white veil. As I watched her move back and forth with a light tread which scarcely touched the ground, the circle she described was cut across by rays from my lamp around which all the moths of the garden were dancing a delirious sarabande. The moon behind the lindens threw into high relief black specters of pine trees that stood immobile in the blue-gray air.

Over the flowers and plants a profound calm reigned. At the first harmonies from the divine instrument the breeze languished, then, falling exhausted on the tall grasses, slowly died. A nightingale had drawn near in the shadows of the foliage and, like the excellent musician he is, had caught the measure and tuned his own ecstatic throat in harmony with the music. He sang on, but as though he had become conscious of rivalry his voice became timid and withdrawn.

We were seated on the steps, listening to strains of the Erl-koenig. As the prelude gave place to the heartbreaking refrain, we sank into the mood of surrounding nature and were engulfed in melancholy enjoyment. And we could not take our fascinated gaze from the magic circle traced before our eyes by the mute sibyl in white. When the music, in a series of sad modulations, merged into tender melody, her steps grew slower.

From that time onward her pace kept the rhythm of the *andante* and the *maestoso*, and her movements showed such marvelous harmony that it was as if the music flowed from her as from a living lyre. Slowly she crossed the lamp-lit space, her white veil forming delicate, distinct contours on the dark background of the picture, while the rest of her was obliterated as it floated into the mystery of night. After a moment she drew near out of the dusk, as if she meant to alight on the white lilac. But, fugitive as the shadows, she slowly disappeared. She did not seem to withdraw under the dark foliage, it was rather as though darkness laid hold of her and drew her into its depths by thickening the curtain of shadows. At the end of the terrace she was completely lost in the pines, to reappear suddenly in the rays of the lamp like some spontaneous creation of its flame. Again she withdrew and floated, vaporous and pale, against the light. Finally she became visible and seated herself on a pliant branch, which supported her weight as though she had been a phantom. Then, as if bound by some mysterious tie to this pale, beautiful woman, the music stopped.

Rising, she glided by an inscrutable mounting movement toward the top of the steps and disappeared into the shadowy hall. A moment later we saw a veritable châtelaine of the middle ages cross the adjoining hall under the light of the candles. Her blond head shone like an aureole, and her veil, thrown over her shoulders, followed cloudlike the light and rapid motion of her flying figure.

The fingers straying across the piano were silent. The lights went out. The vision receded into the night.

June 20.

Up to the 20th, nothing new. Two beautiful storms, weather not so hot. Splendid full moon, horseback rides in the evening with my sister [Madame d'Agoult]. Irresistible desire to let my life go on as it will, without challenging anything, like a lazy wave unconscious (*inconsciente*) of movement.

Piffoël, my friend, *inconsciente* is not French.

My dear friend, what do I care if it is not!

[The next entry in George Sand's journal shows how natural it was for her to accept ideas that were in advance of her times. If it had been written to-day, this dissertation on education would be in no wise remarkable. But when one stops to realize that it is the result of independent thinking on the part of a woman living almost a century ago, it is seen to foreshadow the thought of modern educators. Some of her reflections would do credit to a pupil of John Dewey.

George Sand was intensely interested in education. For months at a time she taught her own children, and the description she has given of her methods shows that she used the technique of what is now called the experimental school. Her criticism of college is not to be interpreted as limited to university education. It is directed to the entire educational system which prevailed in her day, beginning with boys' schools. Against her wishes and in spite of her entreaties, her son Maurice had been placed by his father in a military school at the age of nine years. The discipline which hurt her child's sensitive artist nature infuriated George Sand. When the boy begged to be allowed to stay with his mother, Casimir used his legal authority to refuse permission. At that time, expressing the effect on herself of her child's suffering, George Sand wrote, "I cried until my eyes were bloodshot."]

June 20.

The best education, the only efficient education, said Rollinat the other day, is by the process of *insufflation*.

Then how horrible it is, I said, for a child to be educated at home if he belongs to a family where he absorbs wrong principles and acquires demoralizing habits. Even the abominable régime of college is better than that.

But, on the other hand, if this theory is true, it is the duty of good families to keep the children at home and protect them from college education, because in colleges equality is won by fist fights, discipline is brutalizing, and authority is cruel and puerile—to say nothing of the vices that thrive in such institutions.

Nowadays it seems that moral education is no longer considered necessary. Attention is wholly centered on intelligence, while the heart life is ignored. Our educational system develops pride and self-love in superior children, while it fosters the coarser instincts in commonplace children. In them all, even in strong characters which cannot be entirely corrupted by college education, vanity soon dominates every other quality.

Show me one man in this whole generation who can be cited as an exception to this rule.

The best education would include development of both intelligence and heart. Instruction should be made persuasive and eloquent not by speech alone but by example. The simplest man, the most untutored mother, could nurture a child's affections and implant in his mind ideas of justice, honesty, pride and self-respect.

Firmness should never be excessive or ill-timed. It should be fortified by justice, not by whip and ferule. We ought to take time to reason with a child and explain to him why he is at fault.

More than anything else it is important to understand the child and help the child to understand his own character, so that he may be in harmony with himself. Point out where he has failed and where he is on the right track, keep encouraging him as he makes progress. If the child is avid for knowledge, make it clear to him that intelligence counts for nothing without goodness and love. If the child be lazy and slow but gentle and sweet, make him understand that he should make an effort to apply himself for the sake of those he loves.

Be an impartial critic, show him the absurdity of pretentiousness, affectation, and false modesty. Encourage children to express themselves frankly about whatever they understand. See that pride gets a fall when they boast. Discourage their disposition to dominate. And discourage just as thoroughly the weak self-depreciation that is a pretext for idleness.

Make children realize that they are loved but make them understand, too, that the love of parents is very different from that of friends. Convince them that parental affection will always be there waiting for them, whatever their faults, because the tender affection of parents withstands every test. But make them recognize that the affection of friends is the result of esteem, confidence and choice. Children must learn that friendship is based on merit, and that it is won or lost according as they are strong or weak, devoted to others or egotistically centered on self.

The emulation that develops in connection with these ideas is the only kind worth stimulating. Emulation as it is inculcated in colleges, emulation that tries to snatch from others some vain public honor or ridiculous ovation, is one of the worst sentiments that can be cultivated in mankind. What can be expected of the child who loves to triumph through the defeat of his comrades, or who derives his highest satisfaction from being publicly crowned for having an extra crease in the gray matter of his brain? He will never be more than a jealous poet, a sly, envious artist, or an office-holder infatuated with his silly popularity. He will become a citizen without civic spirit, a patriot because it pays to be patriotic, or an orator more anxious to win applause than to make converts to a good cause. A child motivated by competitive ideals will grow into a man without conscience, shame, or true dignity. He will be useful to himself alone and injurious to others. He will be unhappy, if his vanity is not appeased by success proportioned to his cravings. And if his vanity is thus satisfied he will be despotic and unjust.

[The subjoined fragment reveals that the criticism which had been directed toward George Sand's famous book *Lélia* impels her to arguments of self-defense. In the reviews of the day, *Lélia* was often compared to *Werther, Faust, René, Lara* and *Manfred*. In exonerating the authors of these books and poems it is plain that George Sand indirectly justifies herself, since she was regarded as one of the poets of despair. Following this defense, she again shows her innate tendency to turn her thoughts toward the future. Her imagination, like a searchlight whose rays are projected forward across a dark expanse, enables her to see dimly into the distance ahead. She tries to leap the barrier between her century and our own. She stands, as it were, with us, looking back at herself and her contemporaries.]

June 21.

This exaggerated vanity, encouraged as it is by the system of emulation, and further intensified by social changes of the present century, is responsible for the melancholy pessimism by which so many of our young people are overwhelmed.

Some of our modern critics naïvely believe that youth is corrupted by the influence of certain writers. They point to the author of *Werther* and *Faust*, the author of *René*, or of *Lara* and *Manfred*, and claim that these poets of despair have poisoned the minds of this century. But such a contention is as amusing as a bad joke. It should be taken no more seriously than the theory which attributes the French Revolution to the teachings of Voltaire and Rousseau. I, as a man of letters, have the right to deny positively these miraculous effects of literary productions.

It amazes me to hear critics condemn the influence of poets on their century. It requires the credulous imbecility of a man like Mr. Walsch, or the swollen conceit of our modern *littérateurs*, to thus substitute an effect for a cause. Every age imposes its own emotions and ideas on poetic minds, and by a power like that attributed to God, or formerly to the pythoness, the spirit of the times inspires poets to utter cries of sorrow or impassioned anger.

It is true that popular feelings of revolt or distress acquire greater force when they are made articulate. The poet who finds words for the exaltation or despair of his contemporaries may write the battle song which leads a nation to war, or the funeral dirge which follows dead convictions to their tomb. Nevertheless, the power and value of the poems inhere not in themselves but in the thoughts and feelings of the people to whom they are addressed. The poet who expresses the needs of his century meets a universal response which he does not create. The spirit of the times is summed up, idealized or vulgarized by the poet. He is the alembic in which all the thoughts and feelings of a generation are distilled. He is the tripod to which the pythoness goes when she has oracles to proclaim. He helps to arouse her prophetic agony. But apart from her he is as futile as the serpent's empty skin.

It is not surprising that dull, indolent minds remain unresponsive to the needs of their century. Oblivious to its suffering, they use brutal force to bind it in the iron chains of the past. Their ignorant verdicts, their bombastic fulminations, prove their obstinate adherence to the baseness and injustice of preceding generations.

It is said that our century has achieved progress. If I understand the meaning of this word, it should rather be said that our century is in travail and that in some future time progress will be born. I recognize no progress in the present. I see social turmoil and I believe in the good which will come out of it. Travail and gestation must conform to the laws of nature and bring forth something new. Since this is true, can we fail to be revolted by the narrow minds and barren souls of those who cling to the privileges of inequality as though they were sacred rights granted by heaven?

Must we admit that everything which disturbs the pleasures, habits, sympathies, and even the manias of those who are in power should be called disorder and anarchy? Are we forced to believe that the lords of the earth have learned from their fathers the last word of wisdom? Must we prostrate ourselves before them? Must we stifle in our souls all revelations of truth and deny the lessons of experience? Must we yield to them the sap of life which surges in all men and women? Must we do this solely that we may be imposed upon by these sacerdotal scamps? That would be pitiable. The men and women of the future will laugh cruelly at our cowardice.

They will laugh at us all. They will laugh at our vain efforts toward amelioration, and at the terrible anxiety with which the best-intentioned among us try to do good. They will laugh because we seek far-off remedies when the true remedy is near at hand. They will smile at our inexperience, our doubts, our terrors. Is there anything we do that will not amuse them?

But if these people of the future are better than we are, they will, perhaps, look back at us with feelings of pity and tenderness for struggling souls who once divined a little of what the future would bring.

More than anything else, posterity will laugh at our old fogies of to-day. And, studying this middle century, it will ridicule the morals of our two generations. For it will see old men, whose strength is failing, teach others to continue their vices, while virile young men claim the right to free indulgence in vices of their own.

On the one hand it will see men of the ancient régime. They are the defenders of the monarchy, demanding the people's toil as their time-honored privilege. It will be amused to see that the ancient régime rules by robbery—a robbery that is established, consecrated and ignored.

On the other hand are the upstarts—burglars, brigands and murderers, the men of Philippe, the *nouveaux riches*, who vie with those of the established order for a share of the spoils.

A third group assembles as audience in the arena. These are the children of the century. They are undecided between the old and the new methods of robbery. They look on, trying to discover which of the two is safer and more lucrative.

Shame on us! Is the method chosen by the children of the century to be the discovery we leave to our descendants?

"I am not one of those patient souls who accept injustice with a smiling face."

[It is purely a matter of opinion as to who inspired the mood of sorrow which next finds expression in the journal. One is tempted to attribute the opening paragraphs to thoughts of Michel. But the person referred to in the feminine gender with the adjective "insolent" would evidently be either a servant or a child.

Further passages indicate an emotional disturbance caused by George Sand's children. Since Maurice always loved her, never feared her, and was always spoken of as a comfort and a blessing, the troublesome child was probably Solange. A mother would naturally protect her daughter, even in her journal, by referring to children in the generic sense when she had reason to complain of one child.

Long afterward, when both children were grown and Solange had married, George, having been cruelly treated by her daughter, wrote to Maurice:

"As for your sister, her character is formed now and will never change, so I have reached my decision. The time for suffering and consternation has passed. I have been driven outside myself by suffering on her account, and I have ended by accepting the decree of destiny which in giving me two children has given me but one of my own. The other was born because she had to be. She has lived and will live for herself alone, without the slightest idea of any responsibility to anyone.

"We have tried everything, severity, firmness, leniency, weakness, and, most of all, love and indulgence. Nothing has ever affected her. She has always done whatever she wished.

"To me she is an unknown being. She is, as you have said, incomprehensible. For it is evident that those who live for love cannot understand the interior mechanism of those who do not love.

"I cherish the memory of the little girl who was so beautiful and clever that we both spoiled her. How she always fought against us, and how unhappy she made us, even when she was a child! The young girl was cruel to us, the young woman has broken our hearts."

In the cycle of emotion depicted below, George Sand first reproaches herself for severity and speculates as to whether Piffoël, her masculine self, is in danger of becoming a domestic tyrant. After a few moments of solitude her excitement dies. She feels she has been unduly self-reproachful and realizes that her sympathy for others has been wasted. Then she laughs at herself. Humor helps her to recover her poise. In the end she forgets both domestic worries and inner loneliness in her friendship for the stars.]

June 22.

I have often observed that most people grow bold and hard when they are treated with gentleness and consideration. But as soon as they meet harshness and violence, they lose all self-assertion and become conciliatory and soft. This trait of human nature is almost always apparent in love, and unhappily it often appears in the personal conflicts between friends.

It has always seemed to me contemptible that people should be dominated by fear rather than by love. But, strange to say, this dominance is inevitable. It is necessary to the maintenance of society, and is as essential to the most democratic government as to one of absolute power.

When man is uncontrolled and unrestrained he abuses his freedom. Whoever fears him he despises, whoever loves him he insults. But he fears the one who despises him and loves the one who heaps him with insults. Alexander was honored as a divinity. Jesus received the punishment that is meted out to evil doers. It is still true that by most people goodness is regarded as weakness, while cruelty is respected as force. But human nature is slowly changing. The force and gentleness of to-day are not as extreme as the force and gentleness of the past. Napoleon is more human than Alexander. Sylvio Pellico [1] has none of the divinity of Jesus. I find the conqueror at Saint Helena more appealing than the pretended saint in prison.

Notwithstanding these facts, my own test by which I have been able to judge the most complicated characters is this: "He

---

[1] An Italian writer (1789-1854) who spent nine years in various prisons and wrote the pathetic story of his sufferings in a book entitled *My Prisons*.

who responds to goodness is good. He who yields to force is a coward."

A few moments ago I was obliged to reprimand a person whom I have always believed fundamentally good. But now, after our encounter, I feel that she lacks true dignity. When I spoke to her severely she melted into tenderness and made all sorts of good resolutions. But as soon as I allowed myself to soften toward her, she became hard, opinionated and insolent.

Time and again I have borne on my shoulders heavy yokes of iron. So long as they were placed there with affectionate persuasion and in the name of love and tenderness, I have bowed submissively beneath the beloved hand. But when my friend, grown tired of persuasion, has resorted to commands, when my submission has been claimed, no longer in the name of love and friendship, but by reason of some right or power, I have drawn upon the strength buried in my nature, I have straightened my shoulders and thrown off the yoke. I alone know the latent force hidden within me. I alone know how much I grieve and suffer and love.

Piffoël, Piffoël, what have you to say about all this? You who laugh, grumble and work, you who pretend you are not unhappy and that you have dulled the pangs of suffering. You who always assure me that you haven't time to cry, and that you do not believe in your own pain or in that of others.

Piffoël in your purple robe, how few men have ever caught you in a moment of weakness! But you know by now that I lack your strength. You know that I sometimes break into sobs when I find myself alone with you, while the moon looks on and smiles.

How strong you are, my master! Yet I have known you sublime in tenderness, paternal, persuasive, able to inspire fanatic devotion. You bad old man, have you let your heart grow hard? Do you wish to make slaves of your children? Does the title of master seem to you sweeter than that of father? In this small kingdom your reign is undisputed. Not a hair in your dominion dares to rise against you. At the breath of your anger, those who are near you tremble like leaves in the wind of a storm.

Unfortunate one! The fear you inspire only increases your loneliness. You suffer when you realize that your subjects are cowards. You suffer when you see that they fear and do not love you. You are crushed by the terrible discovery that there is no love where there is no force, and no devotion where there is no resistance.

Slave of your slaves! You cannot leave them. If you lift your iron hand from their heads you will lose their affection. Cease to make them tremble and they will turn against you; cease to be necessary to them and they will let you grow old alone, die alone.

Yet no one has better understood the power of goodness! But man is intoxicated by power and does not know how to curb it. He always demands more, always hopes to find that promised land where flowers and fruits will grow without care and cultivation. And in this search he finds only the desert. There indeed no cultivation is required, because sterile soil cannot be fertilized.

During the last eight days I have been tempted many times to commit suicide. My family responsibilities have seemed to me unbearable. Children, children, you are tyrants, you compel us to live.

But now I have been watching the moon rise. Why do you fear solitude, Piffoël? These few moments of solitude have healed your wounds. You see now that you have done no wrong. Your heart is good and your conscience does not trouble you. Then why all this suffering? Is it because you believe that those who cause your suffering suffer more than you do?

Poor doctor, I alone know how stupid you are. Those whose suffering you pity, weep for themselves alone.

Yes, taking everything into consideration, I believe I have never met anyone as stupidly good as I am. I have a perfect right to say so because my character is naturally violent and self-willed.

But anyhow, if your character is bad, at least you know it. And you do not inflict it upon others. And if you are proud of the goodness which lies at the bottom of your heart you make no parade of it. You hide it so successfully that one must know you very well indeed even to suspect it is there.

Beloved stars, look down on me. I am a tiny speck in a tiny world. I am a poor atom full of love for you, full of faith in you. When you appear in the orient, clothed in robes of gold, I admire your splendor. All night long I worship your glory. I follow your course across the heavens. I watch you drop down toward the other hemisphere. I see you grow more and more mournful until at last, shining like eyes that are full of tears, you are engulfed by dark obscurities of space. Wherever you go, you will find no adorer whose love for you is more ardent than mine.

[The sentiment next attributed to stern Doctor Piffoël might seem more appropriately ascribed to the feminine side of George Sand's nature, were it not for the fact that she inherited her love of birds from a man. Grandfather Delaborde, it will be remembered, sold birds in little cages on the left bank of the Seine. He knew all the bird calls and taught them to his daughter Sophie, who in turn communicated this bird lore to her daughter Aurore.

In her autobiography George Sand relates many charming stories of her experiences with birds. "I am fascinating," she said, "to birds alone." Certainly she had a magical way with them or they would not have been domesticated at Nohant, as they were when the winters were unusually severe.

On one occasion, when she was obliged to lie in bed for several weeks before the birth of Solange, a number of half-frozen birds were picked up by the servants at her behest and given her to resuscitate. Madame Dudevant then deposited the inert birds on a thick green coverlet which had been thrown across her bed. She believed the green bed-spread reminded the feathered brethren of grass or moss, because as they came to life they nestled down on it and seemed to rejoice in its warmth while the storm raged outside. As soon as the storm abated the birds flew away, but the next snowfall brought them back again to seek the same protection.

The picture of George Sand lying motionless under her green coverlet, so as not to disturb the birds on her bed, seems a companion piece for the picture painted here in her journal.]

June 25.

Poor little warbler, how unlucky you were to fall out of your nest last evening before your wings were grown. Forlorn little bird, you are no heavier than a feather and no bigger than a fly. You have made yourself at home here, perching on my finger, nestling in my hair, pecking at my hand and answering the sound of my voice. Who gives you this confidence in my strength, and why do you rely on me to sustain and comfort your weakness? This fold of my sleeve in which you take refuge is not your nest. This hand that feeds you is not your mother's beak. You cannot be so easily deceived, nor have you forgotten your family. You hear the cry of your frantic mother as she hunts for you in the branches of neighboring trees. She would fly through this window if she dared, and you would go to her if you were able. I see that you recognize her cries. Your bright black eyes seem ready to swim with tears. Your head turns restlessly from side to side. Your tiny throat utters feeble notes of protest.

Poor baby bird, you are so fragile that in giving you life, nature seems to have made a jest of you. Yet, that bald head of yours holds a mite of intelligence, and you contain a spark of divinity. You mourn your mother, your brothers, your father, your nest and your tree. You long for a home more suited to your frail organization than the one I provide.

I know that you mourn because you seem troubled. I know you remember because you gaze nervously at the window and feebly strive to answer the voice that calls to you from outside. And since you mourn, since you desire, you love. Yet you submit to the inevitable, and your helplessness is instinct with intelligence which tells you to take refuge in my goodness and to accept my care. You even know how to appeal for sympathy by a manner so full of trust and abandon that it would disarm the hardest heart.

You are not beautiful, I admit. Your ash-colored coat is neither striking nor stylish. Your feathers are ragged. The quills of your tail are rolled into a ball of fur. This manner of dress makes you so dowdy that at first impulse one might be impelled to brush you aside.

Nature distributes her favors unequally. To some of her creatures she gives intelligence, to others beauty. My stupid lap-wing, without sense enough to fly straight, blunders around in a beautiful emerald coat and gorgeous aigrette, while you, aborted bird, are colorless and shapeless, yet you know how to give to your homely exterior all the expression necessary for me to divine your least desire.

The love of weakness for strength is a blessed law of nature, but even more sacred is the love of strength for weakness. Therefore it is that woman cherishes her little ones, and thus man should cherish his woman.

But man, in an effort to maintain and exaggerate the natural dependence of woman, has bound her to himself by laws of servitude. By so doing he has destroyed the joy and the freedom of love.

What woman whose heart life is satisfied will demand a life of intellect? It is so sweet to be loved!

Men mistreat women and abandon them. They despise their ignorance, accuse them of idiocy, and then, when women try to use their own especial wisdom, it is ridiculed. In love, women are treated as courtesans. In the conjugal relation, they are looked upon as servants. Men do not love women. They use them and exploit them, and then consider it fair to subject them to the law of fidelity.

If I abuse you, dear dependent warbler, you will soon escape to the highest trees of the garden, for in a week your wings will have grown and love alone will hold you to my side.

June 26.

Observe the learned doctor now. He has fallen most dreadfully in love. It is high time. He is head over heels at last. The poor distracted man has been unable to write three lines this livelong day. The object of his love has spent her day hopping on his pen, scratching on his paper and doing something worse on his august nose.

Seven times this morning he got out of bed to catch flies and feed them to his loved one. He is as silly as an amorous old man.

Poor Piffoël, where the devil did you pick up such a sweetheart? Your idol weighs about one-seventh of an ounce, she is eight days old, and an extra-big insect's antenna would give her an attack of indigestion that would send her to her grave. Her abbreviated feathers are so few and far between that unless you hold her close to your heart all day, she will die of cold in this warm summer weather.

Piffoël, there is some significance behind all this. Why have you devoted yourself to animals during all the past year? Is this the result of your fierce resistance to the domination of force? Has brute force become so odious, so insufferable, that your soul is rested by a return to the nurture of helpless little things?

Why should this tiny creature seem to you so adorable? I will answer for you, Piffoël.

Because after two days she gave herself into your keeping, without fear. Because she comes at your call and nestles down confidingly in the palm of your hand. Because she trusts your goodness and needs your care. Because you are the only person she knows and loves.

Tell me, Piffoël, is there anyone on earth of whom you can say as much?

June 29.

Overwhelming depression. What is the matter with you, Piffoël?

June 30—July 1.

JULY 1837

Misery, despair, bitter tears. I did not know I loved her so much, poor woman! [1]

July 6.

Good news. The dear soul is getting well.

But your heart is still troubled, Piffoël. What are you worrying about now? What fear of life makes you long for illness and death? This is melancholia, or, to be more honest, it is spleen, the most humiliating thing on earth. Heavens, this wretched human machine! How the mind suffers when the body is out of order. You question everything, you change your opinions a dozen times a day, you see nothing but suffering and injustice in the world—and all because you are constipated. Go on boasting, proud little worm. Drag yourself around. You are as helpless as a beetle whose wings have been pulled off.

[The passage next inserted in the journal seems to be the expression of George Sand's temporary anger toward her husband when, instead of letting her win her law suit by default, he broke his word and brought counter suit, accusing her of every sin on the calendar.

This was the more unfair because George had agreed to divide her fortune with him, and the first arrangement, to which he consented, had been amicable. Legal proceedings against Casimir could not have injured his reputation. He was known only to his neighbors, who were well aware of his bad habits and who accepted them without criticism. George Sand, on the contrary, was known to all the literary circles of Europe. In besmirching her famous name Casimir did not hesitate to accuse her of every form of moral depravity. While none of his accusations were

[1] George Sand's mother, in Paris, was at this time stricken with illness which did not seem to be serious.

proved, they were published in the newspapers. Thus he succeeded in creating false rumors that were never outlived. Some of them persist to this day.

The following entry in George Sand's journal, written in 1836, represents the date of the conclusion of her law suit. Her introductory comment, written a year later, was added to her journal in 1837.]

1837.

The following fragment, found in the bottom of a drawer, has little sense and no value. I preserve it to remind me of one of the most unhappy phases of my life. I was on the border line of madness but I had ceased to brood on the thought of suicide.

1836.

When mental sickness increases until it reaches the danger point, do not exhaust yourself by efforts to trace back to original causes. Better accept them as inevitable and save your strength to fight against the effects.

Try to find the immediate daily causes of these crises. Observe what you are doing or thinking to bring them on. In that way you may prevent them, or at least diminish their force.

When your mental state is normal, try to realize that the delirium is bound to recur. Then when you are delirious, strengthen yourself by the certainty that you will recover your mental poise.

Do not allow yourself to be the dupe of your sick state of mind.

Take care of your bodily health. Eat little at a time and eat often. If your body is accustomed to tonics, take them faithfully. If you are not used to them, do not acquire the habit.

Do not allow yourself to cry. Tears are debilitating. They are followed by exhaustion and other extreme reactions. The only tears that should not be restrained are those of tenderness and compassion.

Above all, above everything, never give way to feelings of anger and vengeance. They are wasteful expenditures of strength.

Human nature is fundamentally good. Yet in spite of our

natural goodness, there are times of stress when we are possessed by rage, and we imagine that by yielding to pent-up emotion we relieve the intensity of our suffering.

The truth is that anger creates anger, just as tears produce more tears. Good and evil cannot be eradicated from our natures. But we can, if we will, repress the evil and express the good.

When vengeance has been overcome by mercy, the softened mood that follows brings a tranquil happiness that is the recompense of victory. It comes from God. Let us accept it and have no fear that we may feel it to excess.

Alas, how seldom we give ourselves the pleasure of rejoicing in ourselves.

Without counting too much upon our strength, we must be confident that strength is in us.

Pray often and humbly, with hope but no certainty that prayer will be answered. For prayer that is merely a demand is no more praiseworthy than the impulse to drink when we are thirsty.

Who has not desired intensely to be delivered from suffering? Who has not cried out in agony: Lord, Lord, hear my prayer! Is mere distress reason enough to be heard? If answer to prayer were automatic, we would never allow ourselves to suffer. There would be no reason for doubt and no merit in faith.

God is not a force outside of us. Nor is he a shining luminary lifted above the skies. Nor is he, in any special sense, the consecrated bread in the chalice of gold.

God is the sun and the skies and the gold of the chalice. He is the bread. He is all the elements of earth. He is the heart of man. He is in us and outside of us. We are in him and never outside of him. He is universal spirit. He reveals himself in man, whom he animates with his breath and whom he sometimes enfolds in his love.

Seek God in man, for as we seek him there, the more transparent the veil of flesh becomes and the more perfectly we learn to find him there.

But we seek him so seldom and so stupidly that we lose all consciousness of God and of ourselves.

If we hold ourselves receptive to the life of spirit, we shall sometimes feel in the depths of our being that mysterious closeness of self and not-self which attests the presence of God in man.

Forgive, forgive the one who has injured you, for the time may come when you will do your own soul an even greater injury, and you may not be able to forgive yourself.

Do not despise weakness in a fellow-being, for you who are strong to-day may awake to-morrow to find yourself weaker than your friend.

Our heaped-up wisdom is not a permanent dwelling place in which we may safely go to sleep. It is a temporary abode in which it behooves us to keep awake, for every day that passes sees at least one stone fall away from the walls we have builded, and at the slightest wind the entire edifice may crumble to the ground.

We do not know what awaits us. Let us learn, then, to dominate the present, or we shall not be able to endure what the future will bring.

[The following somewhat cryptic utterance may be explained by the fact that George Sand was stimulated by a new attraction. The illness of her mother having become serious, George was summoned to Paris, where she stayed for a time. She then took up her abode at Fontainebleau, where she was accompanied by Maurice's new tutor, Félicien Mallefille, who was acting as her secretary. Hearing that her husband, Casimir Dudevant, had threatened to steal Maurice, she despatched Mallefille to Nohant, from which place of danger the boy was brought to Fontainebleau. But Casimir, not to be so easily balked, tore Solange from the protecting arms of her governess and carried her to Guillery, the Dudevant home in the south of France. George went swiftly in pursuit of her daughter. Her companion on this journey was Mallefille. So that the question she asks in regard to Franchard, which she visited with Musset, and Marbore, which she once saw with Sèze, may be answered by the same name, Mallefille.

With the growing detachment which becomes more noticeable year by year, she looks on at her own recuperation from the melancholy of the previous summer and is amazed at her capacity to renew life. "I cannot stop myself," she confesses. Then, feeling more amused than shocked, she reduces her behavior to ridicule. For after giving way to foolish divergations George Sand always found herself absurd.

"To anyone who observes my life superficially," she once wrote to a friend, "I must seem either a fool or a hypocrite. But whoever looks below the surface must see me as I really am—very impressionable, carried away by my love of beauty, hungry for truth, faulty in judgment, often absurd, and always sincere."]

L ET us sum up what has happened during the time that you have stopped observing your own life. Do you recall your melancholy of three months ago? Haven't you completely forgotten what caused it? In the meantime your mother has died, your son has been saved, your daughter has been kidnapped and recovered—and what else! You have revisited Franchard [the gorge in the forest of Fontainebleau] and with whom? You have again seen the Marbore [mountain peak in the Pyrenees] and under what conditions? Now you have returned home. What do you intend to do here? What fate awaits you? Whom will you love? What will you suffer? Whom will you hate next month or next year, or to-morrow? You are as tranquil as though you were contemplating the life of someone else, and you are about to fall asleep in your bed as carefree as Buloz is in his. Your face is as expressive as Enrico's, and your soul is as serene as this silent, peaceful night lighted by the moon and silvered by mist.

What a prodigious soul yours is, O my great Piffoël! If you drank the blood of your children in the skull of your best friend, I doubt if it would even give you the colic. The sun could fall down upon your nose without causing you so much as a sneeze. If Orion left the skies to dance a sarabande on the tops of the pine trees, you would laugh a little, but no more than you laugh at one of Arnal's jokes.

Your *sang-froid* is magnificent. You could eat a piece of granite as though it were a pat of butter, without ever breaking a tooth.

What would you have, my honorable friend? I cannot stop myself. This farce which it pleases you to call my life has the same moral as the legend of the wandering Jew. I am not allowed to die. I am not allowed to rest. I know that my force is inexhaustible, that is why you see me so calm. I know that I must work without cessation, that is why you find me indifferent to what kind of work is given me to do.

I know that I shall never die voluntarily, that is why I no longer pause to count my bad days. Nor do I dream that there are better days to come.

JUNE 1839

[After an interregnum of two years and a half, George comes across her mislaid notebook and recalls that she once intended to keep a continuous journal. The solitude which conduces to introspective writing had been broken by her stay in Majorca with Chopin. She has but lately returned to Nohant. During her absence the notebook had evidently been carried to the attic. She resumes the journal in cheerful mood. But, as is usually the case with problems we try to ignore, her mental worries rise into consciousness and demand expression. Still she attempts to treat them lightly.]

—Do tell me, why haven't you gone on with your journal? (Probably it is Monsieur Three Stars or Madame So-and-So or Mesdemoiselles X.Y.Z. who ask me this question.)

Answer:

—My dear sir, or madame, or my charming young ladies, there are several reasons; but to tell you the most important, I have lost my notebook.

—What! You have carelessly mislaid a book as rare, precious and original as that!

—Even so. And my book is as well bound as it is carefully edited. In fact, the contents are as valuable as the cover.

—Don't joke about anything so important as your notebook. I am sure it is a work of art.

—Ah, you say that to the author!

—Indeed I wish I had found it myself. I would never have given it back to you.

—What the devil would you have done with it?

—I would have cut out all the autographs to paste in my album.

—I don't understand what you mean.

—Doesn't your book contain scraps of handwriting by various authors, artists, politicians, and prominent assassins?

—Yes, I have some rather literary letters, but why do you want them?

—To show that I own them.

—Oh, I understand!

—Besides, why should you wish to keep them for yourself?

—Well, the handwriting helps me to judge people's characters.

—Can you really read character from handwriting?

—Yes, I make a success of it when I know beforehand what the handwriting should prove.

—What would you say of your own?

—My own? I would describe it as tired writing.

—And you conclude?

—That it is the writing of a tired person.

—Is that all?

—Isn't it enough?

—But of what is the person tired?

—Can't you imagine that one may be tired of many things? Tired of getting up every morning, tired of going to bed every night, tired of being hot all summer and cold all winter, tired of hearing innumerable questions asked and never one that is worth answering—

SOLANGE—Look, darling, what book is this? I found it among some rubbish in the attic.

—Good heavens! My thoughts of two years ago in a heap of rubbish!

SOLANGE—Dearest, let me have the book to make paper dolls out of.

—Paper dolls, ruthless child, would you make paper dolls out of my thoughts of 1837?

SOLANGE—Let me look at the pen-marks. Is that the way thoughts are made?

SOMEONE (trying to look wise) —Yes, just like that.

SOLANGE—Well, then, dearest, give it to me to write my thoughts in; I have thoughts, too. I want to write my thoughts.

—Ah, now, I doubt if you have any—

SOLANGE—I have, too.

—Tell me one.

SOLANGE—I love you.

—Tell me another thought.

SOLANGE—I hate Greek history.

—Have you any more?

SOLANGE—I am hungry.

—One more.

SOLANGE—I want to play in the garden.

—Run along, then. That's enough thoughts for one day.

[At this time, June 1839, George is in conflict with her editor, François Buloz, in whose magazine, the *Revue des Deux Mondes*, her novels have been appearing serially for several years.

George needs money. She always needs money. But now especially, after her stay in Spain, and a three months' visit in the south of France for the sake of Chopin's health, her funds are exhausted. The cost of maintaining her household is one thousand francs a month, and her total expenditure, including the expenses of two children and her reckless contributions to Pierre Leroux and other gifted but inefficient friends, amounts to twenty thousand francs a year. Her chief source of income is the *Revue*. The sum of four thousand five hundred francs, which looms so large in the following dialogue, will come to her from Buloz. But first she must earn it by forwarding installments to the magazine for the first and the fifteenth of every month. How many first days and fifteenth days of how many months must pass before she receives the needed money! Financial dependence on her editor irks her very soul. This hateful dependence makes Buloz a terrible figure in her imagination.

Her letters have been full of cries of distress against his slave-driving proclivities. "I break my back to satisfy him!" "Beg him not to press me so hard!" "Overwork is killing me!"—are phrases from her letters to Boucoiran. And from Marseilles, en route from Majorca, she wrote to Madame Marliani, confessing her poverty and explaining the impossibility of securing an advance payment from her editor, "You know Buloz: 'No money, no cash.' " She has sent two manuscripts with instructions to her friend, "He must be made to pay for them on delivery."

Buloz, on his side, is worried by George's growing indifference to romantic love and her increasing interest in religion. "For God's sake, no more mysticism," he implores her. In spite of this touching appeal, George has just completed for the orthodox readers of the *Revue* her unorthodox novel *Spiridion,* the religious opinions of which shock and intimidate her conservative editor.

"Buloz wants," so George complains to Madame Marliani, "innocuous little novels which are equally pleasing to beautiful ladies and to their chambermaids." She adds defiantly, "I shall not write any more of them. I have written too many already"; and concludes, "As for Buloz, who weeps such hot tears when I write what he calls mysticism, let him groan."

As though in repentance for her rebellion, George placated her "brutal" editor by promising to follow *Spiridion* by something "in his own taste." An old novel, half of which had been written immediately after *Indiana* in 1832, was resuscitated and finished. This was *Pauline,* the story of a provincial maiden transported to Paris, where she is seduced, then married, by a rich man. Buloz was delighted with *Pauline,* and friendly relations were temporarily reëstablished.

That Buloz was shrewd and commercial, that he exploited George's popularity in order to build up his magazine, cannot be denied. But his demand for profitable fiction was as inevitable as was George's insistence on her right to her own opinions. Author and editor were approaching a parting of the ways.]

Piffoël, Alone

(*He is in his room, wearing the same dressing-gown he wore in the year 1837, seated on the same sofa, opposite the same table, and his pen still needs to be sharpened.*)

Monologue

Now that my notebook is found, I intend to resume my journal. At the mere sight of it a throng of thoughts come to my mind.

(The specter of Buloz takes shape in a ray of daylight that pushes through the closed shutters. At the vision of Buloz, Piffoël falls prey to frightful agitation.)

PIFFOËL—Lord, what a horrible sight! Go away, dreadful phantom.

THE SPECTER—Four thous—

PIFFOËL—I know what you want, always the same refrain. Go back to the realm of silence, you terrible voice from the tomb.

THE SPECTER—Four thousand five—

PIFFOËL—Stop! I know the rest. Do you want to drain the last drop of my ink, insatiable vampire?

THE SPECTER—Four thousand five hundred—

PIFFOËL—Four thousand five hundred curses!

THE SPECTER—Four thousand five hundred francs.

PIFFOËL—I'd rather say four thousand five hundred masses for the repose of your soul! But have you a soul? Who ever heard of an editor who possessed a soul?

[At the date next inscribed in her journal, George was comfortably established with her children at 16 Rue Pigalle, Paris. Chopin occupied an adjoining apartment and spent his evenings in her salon, to which he brought his music and his friends. Surrounded as she was by Chopin's compatriots, George heard their homesick memories, together with their hopes of redemption for Poland. She absorbed their interests and listened sympathetically to their ideas, especially to those which were impregnated with Polish mysticism.

Adam Mickiewicz, about whom the following story revolves, was George's favorite among Chopin's Polish friends. She felt for him one of those warm, uncritical enthusiasms so often aroused in her by superior, misunderstood men. Mickiewicz was a somewhat visionary leader of his people. As poet, patriot and lecturer he showed the versatility of his gifts and the richness of a temperament whose idiosyncrasies are illustrated in the circumstances explained by George Sand.

The *Dziady* of Mickiewicz was a dramatic poem for which George Sand tried unsuccessfully to find a producer. Failing in her effort to get it staged, she published an article in which *Dziady* was extolled by her as a greater play than *Faust*. This bold claim met such fierce opposition from all critics, great and small, that Mickiewicz became a celebrity in the literary circles of Europe.]

Paris (rue Pigalle, 16), December 1839.

An event which took place a few days ago seems unrelated to the times in which we live.

At a meeting of Polish immigrants a certain mediocre poet, who has a reputation for jealousy, recited a poem addressed to Mickiewicz. In this poem he was generous in praise of Mickiewicz, but at the same time he complained of his own inferiority to the great poet. His self-pity, however sincere, was of course in bad taste. The poem was both a reproach and a eulogy.

The serious-minded Mickiewicz, unconscious of jealousy and indifferent to flattery, arose and improvised a poem, or rather a poetic discourse, in reply. Its effect was prodigious.

No one seems able to describe exactly what happened. Everyone present received a different impression and no two witnesses agree. Some declare he spoke for five minutes. Others insist he talked for an hour. The one thing certain is that he aroused so much emotion that the entire audience fell into a sort of delirium. All over the hall cries and sobs were heard. Some people were hysterical, others declared afterwards that they could not sleep all night. Count Plater returned home in such a state of exaltation that his wife was frightened and concluded he had lost his mind.

Then as soon as he related, not the actual discourse (for no one has been able to repeat a word of it) but its substance and its effect upon the audience, Countess Plater fell into the same strange state which had so alarmed her in her husband. She began to cry and pray and rave.

As a result of this furor, these people are persuaded that there is something in Mickiewicz which makes him almost superhuman. They believe he is inspired like the prophets of old, and their superstition is so compelling that before long they will make a god of him.

Finally I found someone who was able to tell me the theme of Mickiewicz's speech. It was as follows: You blame fate because you are not recognized as a poet, but the fault is in yourself. No one can be a true poet unless he is capable of great love and great faith.

The theme is not without possibilities, and Mickiewicz could and doubtless did make the most of them. He does not remember what he said and he is more disturbed than flattered by the effect his words produced. He admits that something unforeseen and mysterious took place in him. He declares that his speech began calmly, then suddenly he was seized by some emotion that acted upon him like an outside force and he felt lifted above himself. One of his friends who saw him on the following day found him in the state of depression which is the usual reaction from emotional stress.

Listening to these different witnesses and receiving the same testimony from all sides, I seemed to be hearing the description of a scene lifted out of the past. For nothing like this happens nowadays, and in spite of the opinions of Liszt and Madame d'Agoult, it is only in the dilettantism of art that genuine enthusiasm is shown. At least this is true of these modern times. I do not believe in the improvised ardor of our literary pretenders. Our poets and lecturers are all actors. The public applauds them but is not deceived by them. As for our political orators, they are so mechanical that their speeches are made to order and learned by heart.

The effect produced by Mickiewicz is one of those strange exhibitions of power which were once called miracles. To-day we might call them ecstasies.

In his interpretation of religious history, Leroux gives an explanation of these marvels which seems to me the only one our reason can accept. He defines ecstasy as one of the highest faculties of the human mind. His theory will be published some day. In the meantime this is what I have gathered from his writings and from our conversations on the subject.

Ecstasy is for most of us a forbidden force. It belongs to that border land of thought in which the mind of man often finds its most sublime ideas. But if man pushes his thought beyond the farthest limit of that border land, he is thrown into confusion or madness.

Between sanity and insanity there is a state of mind which has never been fully observed or understood. The religious beliefs of all times and all people have accepted it as evidence of man's direct contact with God. It may be called prophetic vision, revelation, the descent of the Holy Spirit, conjuration, illuminism or convulsionism. But, according to the new definition, all these are manifestations of ecstasy.

Leroux thinks our present-day faith in magnetism is the contribution of our atheistic, materialistic century to the age-long tradition of miracle.

Belief in the miraculous is so deeply rooted in humanity that it has survived the loss of religion. Instead of believing in religious power which passes from God to man, we now have faith in the power of magnetism which passes from man to man by the action of nervous fluids. This explanation is no less supernatural than those of the past.

Ecstasy is contagious, as is proved by the history of psychology and by the scientific observations of physiology.

From the descent of the Holy Spirit upon the apostles, to the phenomena of epilepsy at the tomb of Saint-Medard, from the fakir of the Orient to the Passionists of the last century, from divine Jesus and poetic Apollonius of Tyane [1] to the wretched victims of somnambulism, from the pythonesses of antiquity to the nuns of Loudun, from Moses to Swedenborg, one can follow the different phases of ecstasy and see how it is communicated even to those who seem least fitted to receive it.

How does it happen that this state of rapture, which is an essential endowment of great philosophers and poets, is manifested with equal intensity by ignorant men whose minds are under the influence of gross materialism? Is ecstasy merely an illness? Yes, in vulgar minds it may be neither more nor less. But just as fever or intoxication arouse brutishness or fury in base natures, and kindle religious enthusiasm or poetic inspiration in superior minds, so ecstasy develops in each individual the qualities which are peculiarly his own. It may produce miracles of grace, prodigies of superstition, or phenomena of sur-excited animality, according to the nature of those stimulated.

I have met several men who might be called minor ecstatics, but Mickiewicz is the only great ecstatic I know.

However, I would not care to tell everyone that Mickiewicz is splendidly insane, nor would I care to advance the theory that he is suffering from an exalted form of mental illness. But I believe that he shares to some degree the divine madness that is conspicuously noticeable in many illustrious ascetics. This gives him an affinity with Socrates, Jesus, Saint John, Dante and Jeanne D'Arc. But if I went about proclaiming this opinion I would certainly be misunderstood. His friends would be indignant.

Nevertheless, anyone who has a wrong idea of ecstasy might easily call Mickiewicz mad, after reading certain passages in *Dziady*. And if he compared these passages with Mickiewicz's

[1] Pythagorean philosopher who died in the year 97. His so-called miracles were considered by the pagans equal to those of Jesus Christ.

well-reasoned lectures in the College of France, he might easily conclude that the lecturer was an impostor.

He is neither unbalanced nor a poseur. He is a big-hearted man, full of genius and enthusiasm, completely master of himself, and able to maintain his own point of view with poise and logic. But sometimes he is carried away by the nature of his beliefs, by the violence of his elemental instincts, and by the sympathy he feels for the misfortunes of his country. He has the prodigious élan of a poetic soul whose forces are not inhibited. There are times when these forces precipitate him into that border land between the finite and the infinite where ecstasy begins.

The terrible drama which takes place in the soul of a poet has been described in *Konrad* with a power and truth which make the book a masterpiece. No one who has read *Konrad* can deny that Mickiewicz is ecstatic.

[George now turns her attention to her friend Heinrich Heine. The sympathy she expressed for him in her journal was felt in turn by Heine for George Sand. Women who talked against her were classified by him as "malicious cats who caressed her with one paw and scratched her with the other," while her male detractors he referred to as dogs baying at the moon. Of George herself he said, "Like the moon, she smiles down at the dogs who bark at her."

Heine, according to Madame Karénine, fell in love with George Sand on first acquaintance. About a year was required for his recovery, after which he became George's devoted friend and always addressed her as "Dear Cousin." Shortly before his death, when poverty and sickness had accentuated his bitterness, he behaved to George like the dogs he had decried, accusing her of an absurd *liaison* with a man who was his pet aversion. No doubt there was some obscure reason for linking her name with that of a man he hated. When this unpleasantness occurred, the invulnerable George continued to smile down on Heine's barking like the kind and gentle moon she had once seemed to him. Hearing his accusations she made no self-defense, but in defense of her unhappy friend she explained his gossip by saying, "Genius is given to morbid imaginings."

Both Heine and George were poetic souls living in an inimical world. Heine was sarcastic when he was hurt, George grew cynical when she suffered. It was especially in her friendships with women that George felt the need and the lack of understanding. The following paragraphs illustrate the kind of women by whom she was surrounded. Her feeling against neglectful mothers was, as will be recognized, a deep resentment.]

January 7.

Heine can say diabolically clever things. Speaking of Alfred de Musset this evening he said, "He is a young man with a brilliant future behind him." Heine's witticisms hurt because his arrows always hit the mark. He is considered inherently wicked, but nothing is farther from the truth. His heart is as good as his tongue is naughty. In love he is tender, romantic, and soft even to weakness, and he is capable of endless submission to a woman's domination. Nevertheless he is a cynic and a mocker. His talk is so materialistic that he scandalizes those who do not know his private life and the secret of his household. He is, like his poetry, a mixture of exalted sentimentality and clownish mockery. He is a humorist, like Stern and like my friend the Kill-joy [Jules Néraud]. As a rule I do not care for sarcastic people, yet I have always loved these two men. I have never been afraid of them and I have no cause to complain of them. They are inclined to make fun of queer people, but their sensitive natures have a poetic, generous side which responds to sincerity and friendship. They are badly behaved men whose true natures are good. They are bad only in bad company.

To tell the truth, that thin, sharp, affected little woman whom —— has married is more terrifying to me than the worst satirist on earth. I am afraid of her because she is envious and mean, because her mind is as insignificant as her nose, and her heart as cramped as ——'s; because she does not and cannot understand anything or anybody. The most innocent action strikes her as a crime. Friendliness is interpreted as animosity, indifference becomes a menace. Her personality is vulnerable at every turn; then, in order to defend herself and avenge herself, she talks against others. But as she cannot see straight and gets everything upside down, her criticism becomes calumny. All this goes on in her unconsciously.

One should protect one's self from such women as from a pestilence, and never let them get so much as a glimpse into one's private affairs. Not that one gains anything by it, for what they do not know they manufacture, but at least one need not reproach one's self with having furnished them with the material. Everything in their conversation is false, even to appearances.

Madame Y. is a woman of the same type, with an even greater inclination toward perfidy and downright malice. All three are eaten by envy and consumed by despair at not being loved. Poor things! Poor wretched women!

For some time I have had an antipathy for Madame C., though I admire one side of her character. She alienates me by her pettiness, then wins my respect by her bigness. She is a small, thin woman. She is not well formed and does not carry herself well. But she is pretty just the same. Nature has endowed her with dimples in her cheeks and a smile that redeems her entire personality. La Touche used to say that she was a pretty little rose-colored pedant. Chopin calls her a school-boy in petticoats. Six years ago she had superb ash-blond hair. It turned brown in Italy, and brown hair is very becoming to her. I am sure she does not dye it, because she is not much of a coquette. In fact she is not enough of one, for she is altogether lacking in feminine appeal, and with the exception of Buloz, who has loved her for a long time and very badly, I have never known a man whom she pleased.

It seems to me that if I were a man she would please me, for I do like women without affectation, and she is absolutely natural. She is a singular being. In spite of her fine qualities she is full of contradictions and inconsequence. Perfidious without being mean, pedantic without vanity, erudite without real knowledge, serious without depth, always trying to get to the bottom of everything, she remains superficial. She has fulfilled the duties of a mother, yet she does not seem to have room in her heart for the least trace of tenderness for anyone on earth. Her life is full of love affairs and she talks continually of her loves and passions. She will recite her agonies to you in the most serene contented tone. She confesses her lapses in a manner that is coldly cynical. In theory and in practice she has a principal love in her life, and takes on casual lovers to kill time and quiet her nerves. It is not pleasant to hear her when she gets on this subject, for though she is mentally detached and has a quite original candor, she seems to have no feeling, no enthusiasm, no tenderness.

In conversation she turns abruptly from her love affairs to history, philosophy, religion and politics, all of which she discusses with cool exuberance and frivolous erudition. Then all of a sudden she gets up and leaves you, to go nurse her baby. The child is, according to her own description, coarse, ugly, strong, and wicked, and, as she herself says, "like the brutal passion which created it."

Last year while Madame A. was in Italy she wrote Madame B. a long letter devoted to inquiries about dresses and hats. Then as a postscript she added: "By the way, I forgot to tell you that I was confined last month at Rome—a boy—I left him there. Madame C. did the same."

But Madame C. did not do the same. She had a child on her own account, it is true, but there is this difference between the two women—Madame C. keeps her children, nurses them, rears them, gives them her name, her time, her life, while the other abandons and forgets hers. She lets her children be brought up in a hovel, while she herself goes clothed in velvet and ermine. She is nothing more nor less than a kept woman, and no more concerned with her offspring than if they were a litter of kittens.

[After giving her opinion of certain types of women for whom she felt contempt, George Sand now speaks in her journal of a woman she admires.

Pauline Garcia Viardot came of a family noted in music. Her father, Manuel Garcia, was a Spanish singer and composer, while her older sister, Maria Felicia, became the famous singer and actress, Madame Malibran. Both by training and inheritance Pauline was a thorough musician. Very early she won distinction as a concert singer, and later in life on the grand opera stage. Pauline was more remarkable for intelligence than beauty. Her features were heavy, but the brunette coloring of her distinctive type gave her a striking appearance more interesting and original than a pretty face.

She was, at least, alluring enough to attract the attention of Alfred de Musset. Imagine George Sand's consternation—her cherished friend about to fall a prey to the deadly charm of Musset! For that he was still fatally fascinating George had not a doubt.

As soon as this gossip reached her ears, George's protective sense was aroused. How could an innocent child guard herself against the advances of an erotic poet whose notorious unfaithfulness had already broken so many hearts? There was poor young Aimée d'Alton who had trustingly given herself to him, only to be discarded. There was also the actress Rachel, to whom he was openly paying court. Was Pauline to share the fate of Aimée? Would she be forced to compete with the great Rachel for a share of the polygamous poet's heart? George stood ready to protect her protégée.

But the danger she feared existed merely in her own imagination. Unlike George, Pauline was neither impressionable nor romantic. At seventeen, the age at which she met Musset, she had been far more sensible than George had been at twenty-nine when Musset came into her life. Besides, Musset was now a trifle jaded and very dissipated. Healthy-minded Pauline felt an instinctive aversion to the French Don Juan. She found him, as she confided to a friend, "very arrogant, even repellent, especially when he looked at women. His red-lidded eyes," she noted, "had no lashes, and his face was totally lacking in eyebrows. Often," she continued, "he stares at a woman so fixedly that one is frozen by the insolence of his bold cynical gaze."

Like a wise and prudent child, Pauline Garcia fastened her young affections on a good man who could be useful to her career. Louis Viardot, twenty years her senior, had means and leisure which enabled him to devote his life to a talented wife. After their marriage he traveled about with her on her concert tours, and, since he was a cultured man and something of a *littérateur*, he meanwhile devoted his own ability to writing books on the literature of Spain.

George had done her best to encourage this appropriate marriage, and the Viardots were grateful for her aid. Writing from Rome on their honeymoon, both bride and groom addressed her as "our good angel," while the bride signed herself "Your devoted daughter, Pauline."

One notices in George's journal that Pauline's common sense was at times a trifle baffling to her mother by adoption. But George thoroughly recognized the child's remarkable gift, and prophesied for her the brilliant success which she ultimately attained. Pauline had a voice of remarkable range. She sang with equal ease contralto, mezzo soprano, and high soprano. This latitude enabled her to play in turn all the chief rôles of Italian opera.

The character Consuelo in George Sand's novel by that name was, as the author admitted, drawn in large part from her study of Pauline Garcia, although Consuelo borrowed something also from George's knowledge of the greater musician, Franz Liszt. When a copy of *Consuelo* reached Pauline in Spain, where with her devoted Louis she was on concert tour, Pauline wrote to George: "*Consuelo* made us tremble, laugh, weep, and reflect. I cannot tell you what has taken place in me since I read *Consuelo*. I only know that I love you ten thousand times more than ever, and that I am very proud to have been one of the composite bits which have helped you to create this splendid character. No doubt it will stand as the best thing I have done in this world!"

George's friendship with Pauline continued as long as she lived and deepened with the years. It is scarcely necessary to add that the emotional crisis anticipated by George in her vision of Pauline's future never arose. This fantastic vision illustrates the swift functioning of George's imagination. Some slight detail, the mention of a name, was enough to give wings to her fancy. Once started, her imagination was soon beyond control, it carried her along until, as in this instance, she landed in the clouds.]

January 18, 1840.

Day after to-morrow Pauline leaves for London. I cannot say that I am sorry. She must follow her vocation, her purpose in life. But I should be sorry if I thought I should never see her again.

She is the only woman I have greatly loved in ten years. She is the only woman I have loved without reservations since I parted from Sister Alicia in the convent. More than that, I believe she will always be the only woman I can love with certainty and admire with reason. She is a child of nineteen, however, and I doubt that the chasm between our ages can be overcome. No, I do not believe it can ever be bridged.

She seems to me endowed with a strong mind which will protect her from excessive emotion and prevent her from giving much sympathy to the emotions of others. Even while she is at the age to fall in love, she will never lose her head nor understand the love madness of those who are less poised.

Her being is complete, well organized and expressive. What will life mean to her? Art, nothing but art. At least that is my prophecy. But what do I know about it?

It seems to me that I give Pauline the same indulgent love I give my son and daughter. And to this tenderness I add the admiration her genius inspires. Does she love me in return? Fortunately that is not necessary to my happiness. My feeling for her bears no resemblance to the foolish admiration I seem to have inspired in the daughter of ———. What she felt for me was a sort of infatuation which repelled me. She is abnormal and my Pauline is good.

I also am good, no matter what they say. And what they say does not bother me. No injustice that is shown me troubles me. The truth is, I am never repelled by what is natural. Whatever belongs to the order of life seems to me beautiful and right.

This child will not care very much for me because she will never understand me. The only person who means a great deal to her at present is her husband. She loves him with tenderness, kindness, and tranquillity. She has had no experience of the madness, intoxication and suffering which mean passion.

Great artist, may you know no love other than this you feel to-day. It is the only love permanently satisfying—still, it is not the only possible love.

As long as you realize no other, I shall be useless as a friend to you. God forbid that you may need my friendship, because if you ever turn to me for sympathy it will mean that you suffer more than your fine nature deserves. It will mean that there is an enemy at your right and an enemy at your left. You will be surrounded by enemies, and among them will be your husband, your lover, and all the prying people of this vulgar-minded world.

If that day came, perhaps no one except me would cherish you as you are used to being cherished, no one else would realize how worthy you are of respect.

I might even die before she is subjected to so great a trial. If so, may the Lord send her someone else who loves and knows and comprehends her as I do.

Man and woman, law and nature, marriage and love!

AN ARGUMENT AGAINST ABSOLUTE INDIVIDUALITY

Among the important arguments which might be urged against the doctrine of absolute individuality, there is one very small argument which I will set down here. It is based on a fact of observation.

Have you ever met a person who seemed to you entirely new and unknown? Because that has never happened to me. When I meet a total stranger my first impression is that I have seen him somewhere before. I try to remember where it was we met. I try to recall his name, and I wonder why he has so greatly changed since I last saw him. By the time I have reached the conclusion that I do not really recognize this seeming acquaintance, I begin to search my memory for the person whom he resembles so closely as to have caused my mistake.

Sometimes I make the connection very quickly, for every man has a double or two in this world. And this double has his double, who also has his, although usually they do not know one another.

This resemblance may be vague, remote, mysterious. The more it baffles, the more it torments me. Even when I do not care for the stranger himself nor for the person he looks like, I still care about the resemblance and am driven to find it. But when it is found it is so imperfect that I wonder how I was able to trace it.

Sometimes the likeness between a stranger and a friend is so indefinite that I must recall an intermediary person whom both resemble. When my memory discovers him, the connection between the two others is established. He relates them to himself and so to each other.

The intermediary may be attached to the two dependent personalities by means of other intermediaries who depend on him and on one or both of the others. Thus the connection is established in my memory by a chain of divergent types all of whom suggest the principal type. This more or less elaborate process of association will then explain why, at first impression, the unknown person did not seem unknown to me.

Sometimes the resemblance is suggested by the features, sometimes by the voice, manner, posture or expression or by all of these taken together. Sometimes it is suggested by several characteristics, but never by less than two, otherwise the likeness would be too indistinct to convince me.

For I insist that this is not at all a matter of imagination but one of experience.

My interest in these analogies may be childish but it is involuntary and imperious. It is useless to suppress it, because when I try to accept anyone as an identity detached from the long chain of those I have known, I suffer more than is endurable. In fact, an individual irritates me until I succeed in making him a link in my chain. This method of association is the touchstone of my spontaneous sympathies and of my sudden and invincible antipathies.

My memory is so fortunately organized that it buries in oblivion the names and faces of those who have been offensive to my mind or heart. After a time I am freed of them because for me they cease to exist.

Nature has presented me with a valuable gift in my instinctive distaste for personal resentments. That is why first impressions disturb me more than memories. I fear the people to whom I cannot quickly say, Oh, you! I know you, I like you. You belong to the family.

How many times in some one's drawing-room, or in a shop, or on the street, I have run across people the mere sight of whom has made me tremble or has even made me feel ill. They have, of course, been wholly unconscious of their effect on me. They seemed like evil spirits escaped from a previous existence in which I had been their victim. In meeting them I feel myself in danger of being recognized. I fear they intend to pursue me again in this life. And all because their faces suggest some suffering I once endured.

But as soon as I discover the one they resemble, I no longer am frightened, nor am I repelled. Why should I be afraid of anyone who can be recognized and known? He is unmasked. Suppose that he reminds me of some one in whom my confidence was misplaced. Very well, a wall is between us forever. But I no longer fear him. I wish him well and dismiss him from my mind.

At the other extreme of experience there are faces that inspire me with veneration. And for me there are tones of the human voice that have an immediate, compelling charm. A fleeting expression on the face of a stranger will win my sudden, complete

confidence, or his smile will win my heart because he reminds me
of a friend who is absent or of one who is dead.

But, you will say, an outward likeness bears no relation to an
inner similarity of character, which is a different matter altogether.

True, I do not jump to the conclusion that an apparently good
man is a rogue because he has one feature which reminds me of
some villain I once knew. Nevertheless that feature may suggest
something that pertains to the villainous character, not neces-
sarily his chief vice, but some weakness, like vanity or love of
wealth. It may even suggest a slight tendency toward the dominant
vice, although the tendency may have been overcome by difference
in education or by the balance of certain fine qualities which the
villain lacked.

Therefore if the resemblance is striking, it might be well to be
on your guard. Do not place too much confidence in the good man
who resembles a villain. And see that you do not lead him into
temptation.

But all this is merely to illustrate the truth that there is no
absolute individuality. No one is isolated and alone.

There are typical characters who are brothers to one another
or who are children of the same type. They are tied to one
another by a thousand little filaments. The whole human race is
a network of which every man is a thread. Of what use is a bit of
thread separated from the whole mesh? Where the stitches are
broken the fiber is destroyed.

The blood relation of the members of the universal family
leaves indelible imprints on their faces. In vain do we try to
repudiate our relatives. From the cradle of the human race up to
the present day, nature has been laughing at our efforts to stand
alone.

January 1840.

Will any method of persuasion reach those who are set against the truth? What goes on in their minds? Tell me, Lord, that I may learn to understand them. What appeal can be made to minds protected from truth by an iron wall of prejudice? Are there men who cannot forsake their errors? Is there an age beyond which the mind cannot change? Base and cowardly natures instinctively hate truth and justice. That we know and accept. But what are we to think of human nature when we meet noble minds which are open to truth on many sides, and see them close before a phase of truth which offends their prejudice?

"I cannot believe" seems to be the ultimate word of this age. Yet faith has been the root of all religions. Is there no middle ground between those who remain blindly attached to the past, and those who try to tear down everything without allowing anything to be saved?

Is it true that the seeds of truth are sown only in the souls of those who are called ignorant? Must the people who call themselves "enlightened" perish from the face of the earth, carrying with them their errors and resistances? Must the dead be sent once again to bury their dead?

PREFACE

THIS large scrapbook, which bears the English title *Sketches and Hints*, is bound in natural-colored leather.

George Sand consigned to it some of her cherished souvenirs and ideas.

It contains personal impressions, letters, and echoes of conversations. What gives to this intimate collection its greatest interest is the fact that George Sand reread the fragments she had jotted down during various phases of her past, and from a height above her tumultuous existence judged herself and the life she had led. Her vision became ever clearer, broader, and calmer.

AURORE SAND

SKETCHES AND HINTS

[Of George Sand's two poems whose meaning, without the rhyme or rhythm of the originals, is given in the following translation, the first was written at the age of thirteen, and the second at twenty-eight.

There is one interesting fact about the poems; although separated by a distance of fifteen years, they are fundamentally alike. Both reveal George Sand's temperamental melancholy, her inescapable loneliness, and the mysticism which was the essence of her being and which alone gave identity to the different kinds of women she became. Everything else in her changed, but as she outgrew each former self, her unalterable mysticism linked together the little Aurore, Mademoiselle Dupin, Madame Dudevant, George Sand, Madame Sand, and Grandmother Sand.]

VERSES WRITTEN AT THE CONVENT

As night throws down its shadows
Like black palls shrouding the monastery walls,
My dreamy soul is drawn to you,
O moon, mournful lover of the tomb.

Guide my steps with your dim white light,
As I wander through these cold marble halls.
Here I await, without haste or dread,
The end of my short pilgrimage.

Sheltered from life in this holy retreat,
Already I resemble the dead,
For my heart has lost its last desire
And knows neither pleasure nor pain.

As the heavens are unclouded,
So my soul is undisturbed;
Soon I shall sleep in the peace of the grave,
And for me no friend will mourn.

AN AUTUMN NIGHT, 1832

The love I bear you, Kreyssler,[1] is like a dream of the night
Which disappears in the light of morning,
A dream that is lost all through the daytime,
But that, as soon as night returns,
Starts my heart beating again
With the hope that some day
    I may know happiness.

So long as I hold this illusory hope
I am lulled into peace;
So long as I stay in the realm of dreams
My suffering is drugged.
But the voice of fate awakens me, saying,
God's promise of rest will soon be fulfilled,
    But for you that rest is death.

Try, beloved Kreyssler, try to rekindle the fire
Of my dying soul.
Can you bring me back to life?
Too late! The wind has already effaced
That note of faith and hope
Which your consoling voice sent into space—
    Happy are those who can love!

[Shortly after the second poem was written, George Sand returned to Nohant, taking with her Solange, who had been established with her mother in Paris. Solange was almost four years old now; the boy Maurice was nine.

[1] Kreyssler is one of Hoffmann's heroes.—*Aurore Sand.*

The reason for this trip to Nohant in August, 1832, was the usual one—Maurice's school vacation, which he was to spend with his alienated parents. The child was supposed to be too young to realize their estrangement, and while the arrangement was far from satisfactory to the mother, it enabled her to share with Casimir the son whom she adored. The woman who is so often called "a law unto herself" never achieved complete independence, because she refused to abandon her children. At this period she had been living in Paris for about a year and a half, but every alternate three months were spent at Nohant. On these brief visits to her former home it was punishment for her to live as an unwelcome guest in the house where she had been mistress. It was painful also to renew old ties which had been outgrown and yet could not be broken.

In spite of her newly won success—*Indiana* had been published three months earlier—all George Sand's letters of this period are very melancholy. Those to François Rollinat dwell upon her wretched domestic situation, while her correspondence with Émile Regnault shows her waning enthusiasm for Jules Sandeau. The unhappy woman was already aware that her union with Jules was likely to end as disastrously as her marriage. Surrounded by wounding associations, depressed, as she felt, about Jules, what more natural than to revive the memories of their first meetings in those very woods, on that very bench, where his boyish love had been shown before it was confessed? How inevitable also the vague fears of approaching separation from her lover, forebodings which were soon to be realized, as the break between them occurred four months later.

To whomever George Sand addressed the following communication, whether to Jules or to some other friend or former lover, on rereading the letter at a later date she cut out the passages which would have identified the man—it must have been a very young man indeed—who cut his initials on a tree. That the letter was not sent is evidenced by the presence of the moss she enclosed.

The simplicity and tenderness of this withheld message is conveyed in George Sand's own natural style, which she adopted when she forgot the demands of public taste and wrote for herself alone or for a close friend.]

PERSONAL RECOLLECTIONS

September 11, 1832.

IT is love, not faith, that removes mountains.

Yesterday I followed the old path I used to take to the vineyard. All its beauty has gone. Where is the lost verdure of these once lovely fields? Where are the youth and poetry that once gave life to this river? Everything has been devoured by the summer drought. No grass nor wild thyme is on the hillside, no mint lifts its head along the water's edge. There are places where the stream has been dammed for the sake of the millers, and the precious water, forcibly held, has become stagnant and green. It smells. It exudes an oily decay. The water lilies that grew in it are dead.

I walked half way up the hill and drank at the little spring in the middle of what used to be a meadow. But now the field has been plowed, so that to reach the spring you must wade across a stretch of dry barren ground where your feet sink into soft earth.

But the spring remains clear and sweet. Around it little clumps of reeds have saved it from the drought. It flows on with the same old plaintive song, and still has the delicious flavor of peppermint and aromatic herbs. It lives, surrounded by devastation, like a soul that stays pure in the midst of depravity.

Opposite this bubbling fountain, you remember, there was a bridge across the road. This was the road I took to Montgivray. At the end of the same path was another bridge, made with a ladder on top of which a board had been placed. Do you remember how it wobbled under our feet, that frail little bridge? how gayly the water rippled over the pebbles, how cool and shady it used to be?

There is neither board nor bridge now. There is hardly any

river. The mill wheels do not even turn round. They are over-grown with grass and moss. The trees have no more leaves. You lucky ones who went away did well to transport your nest and your loves elsewhere. This dreadful weather would have driven you away by now.

At the end of the ravine, you remember, a thick group of trees concealed the path and shielded your trysting place from the eyes of the passer-by. Someone has ruthlessly chopped off the branches of those trees. I looked for the one on which you had cut my initials. It has gone.

I came back by the open path where the big elm stands. How often, with dusty feet and shoes torn by stones, I have walked that path! And though the sun blazed down on my head, my heart was singing and my step was light. How happy I was! How young we were! And how empty, sad, and disenchanting all this countryside is now! Ah, well, there is an end to everything. It is foolish to care too intensely for the places where one has been happy. Happiness takes wings, places change, and the heart grows old!

* * * * * * *

. . . Half-felt emotions and half-hearted forgiveness we will leave to others. Between us a serious break could never be patched up. The more unreservedly one has loved, the more one is driven to hatred when the heart that has been trusted is poisoned by ingratitude.

* * * * * * *

. . . The big drawing-room is so cold that it is closed and we use the yellow room instead. I stay there an hour after dinner, playing with my children, then I return to my study and the children follow me, for to the great disgust of Boucoiran they prefer me to him. Maurice writes stories, dialogues, proverbs, skits, iambics. His complete works fill at least fifty notebooks. The pages are numbered, there are tables, references, footnotes, sketches and headings in ink. He is ruining me by his reckless use of paper, ink, drying powder, etc. His sister jumps on my bed and prances up and down on it like a colt. While this is going on, I work.

I spent my entire morning in the little wood. The day seemed like spring except for the lack of budding leaves and nightingales. However, winter has its own charms, scents soft as violets, and fresh green moss which covers the tree trunks like a garment to shelter them from cold.

Rain has pounded on the old bench until it has plowed it with diminutive furrows that now feed a rich vegetation in every crevice. I am sending you one of its most vigorous plants. At this moment it is very green, but by the time it reaches you it will be faded.[1]

I explored the wood to-day in every direction, retracing the past. I began with my earliest memories. Did I ever show you the place where my mother made a garden? She planted rose-bushes there, then with mossy stones and pebbles which were gathered from the river, she cleverly constructed a grotto where I could sit in the shade. She even managed the semblance of a spring, made by a bowl full of water sunk in the ground up to the rim which was hidden by violets and shells. All this seemed to me a marvel of beauty. I spent the better part of every day on my grassy couch beside the grotto. There I used to take my bowl of cream for breakfast. There I read *The Ass's Skin* and *The Blue Bird*. In those days I was brown like Maurice and rosy-cheeked like Solange. My mother was good to me then, and life was serene and happy. I was five years old.

There is another spot in the woods which brings back to memory the time I was twelve years old. At that age I was strong enough to clear a path through the thicket with my knife. I had to cut through innumerable interlaced twigs of privet and honey-suckle. Deep in the woods, completely concealed, I found an old

[1] Some bits of moss are stuck to the page with green wax.—*Aurore Sand.*

tree. On it I hung necklaces made of colored shells. Beside the tree I made a seat of moss. There I could hide away during all my free hours to read in peace. Even then my chosen books were serious. There I read my first poets and spent delightful hours with the *Iliad* and *Jerusalem Delivered*. Often I would dream, arms folded, knowing nothing, vegetating, feeling myself grow with the grass I trod underfoot.

Maurice shows all my tendencies. He has to-day the same character I had then. In watching his life unfold I seem to be rereading my own.

[The three months' visit to Nohant was completed in November, 1832, when George Sand returned to Paris to move from Place St. Michel to an apartment at Quai Malaquais. Now for the first time she enjoyed the luxury of carpets, a porcelain stove, and a servant for Solange.

A room in this apartment was set aside for Jules Sandeau. But their happiness together was short-lived. In January, 1833, Jules proved unfaithful. Then the prophecy, "a serious break between us could never be patched up," was fulfilled. George could not forgive Jules, although she generously paid his expenses for a trip to Italy.

After Jules' departure she lived alone, converting her melancholy into a long prose poem in novel form, called *Lélia*. In March part of the book was read to the foremost critic of the century, Sainte-Beuve, who then sent her a letter expressing so much admiration that it was enough to turn her head. The influence of such encouragement might well have determined an ambitious woman to dedicate her life to creative work.

But George Sand, having received Sainte-Beuve's prophecy of the brilliant career that awaited her, behaved like any other woman whose heart needs are more imperative than any desire for fame. Soon afterward she met Alfred de Musset and plunged into the disastrous affair which deflected creative effort from her work. If she had denied her emotions and devoted her life to work alone, would she have been more or less of an artist? More or less of a woman?

No book she ever wrote brought George Sand so much fame as

Lélia, which was the outcome of a period of solitude and suffering. Gustave Planche, literary critic of the *Revue des Deux Mondes*, said of *Lélia*, "It is this century's analysis of itself. It is the agonized cry of a society which has denied God and truth, only to look into its own heart and find that its dreams are illusions."

George herself admitted of this book, which was written when she neither loved nor was loved, "*Lélia* is the novel in which I have put more of myself than in any other book."

George Sand had met Sainte-Beuve two months before his letter in praise of *Lélia* was written. He had reviewed *Indiana* and *Valentine*. It was to thank him for his commendation that she had asked Gustave Planche to bring the distinguished critic to call. At this first meeting Sainte-Beuve was somewhat discomfited to find that the virile author who used the pen name George Sand was only a quiet little woman. Except for her marvelous eyes, he saw in her personality no suggestion of the power and brilliancy proved by her pen. He expressed surprise at finding her so plainly dressed.

After this first meeting the great man called on Madame Dudevant occasionally. Their relations were cordial but formal. He was a little afraid of her. Each time he puffed and panted his way up the steep stairs that led to her apartment he found her less baffling and less intimidating, until, on the evening preceding the writing of this letter, he had, somewhat timidly, begged permission to call himself her friend.

One can easily imagine the visit in George's small salon, on the evening of March ninth. Sainte-Beuve, short, fat, homely almost to ugliness, was self-consciously wondering whether the mysterious creature whose terrifying cleverness was hidden behind so simple an exterior was secretly criticizing his defects. George, homely diffident, far from feeling critical, had begun to revere the chubby little man of whom she wrote, "Sainte-Beuve is the man I respect most. There is something in his soul which suggests an angel, while his naïve and obstinate character is like that of a child."

Seeing her book near completion, she was full of gloomy foreboding as to its reception by the public. *Lélia*, begun as a journal, had taken shape as a novel of symbolic characters. George's uncertainty about the value of this bold experiment, Sainte-Beuve's eager curiosity, the interest he always displayed in a forthcoming

ook, broke down her habitual reserve. She read the closing pages
of her soul's despair, and the prince of critics listened to the low
mpassioned voice.

The next day, under the spell of a new enthusiasm, he wrote the
etter which she treasured all her life.]

A LETTER FROM SAINTE-BEUVE TO GEORGE SAND

March 10, 1833.

MADAME:

I cannot restrain my impulse to tell you of the deep impression
made upon my mind by what you read to me last evening. *Lélia*
sustains and intensifies the great admiration and friendship I feel
for you. I shall not attempt to discuss *Lélia* as a book or finished
work until you are good enough to let me read the first part.
But it is not difficult to imagine what that is like. The big public,
which is everlastingly asking for stories and nothing but stories,
will reject it, but those who regard the novel as the best medium
for vivid expression of universal and eternal thought will give to
the author of *Lélia* a very high place. It will be accepted as your
book of philosophy, your general survey of human relations and
life. All your novels that are to follow will be illumined by *Lélia*
as by a light from above. It will give to them a profound authority
which otherwise they might not have attained for many years.

But apart from all consideration of *Lélia* as a literary achievement, and regarding it solely as a revelation of her who conceived
and expressed it, I can never make you realize how amazed I was
by the sureness of touch, the continuity of thought, and the
sustained power with which you carry one across regions so wide
and deep that at every step he who follows you is frightened and
dizzy.

To be a woman, to be less than thirty years old, and yet, without showing any trace of these limitations, to have sounded every
abyss of thought; to bear the weight of an amount of wisdom

which would make a man's hair fall out or turn white, to bear it lightly, easily, without loss of poise—that is what I admire in you.

The Lélia I admire most of all is the Lélia in yourself, in the essence of your soul, in what you have slowly reasoned out and felt. How powerfully you express her when you let go of yourself in writing! How well you know how to conceal her under the simple exterior of your everyday life!

The truth is, Madame, you are a rare, strong soul. And if in this book your thought and feeling seem at times embittered, it is only the wine in the chalice which has shown itself corrosive, while the chalice itself, of unalloyed metal, remains virginal and unspoiled.

Whether or not your heroine continues to despair, life offers you consolation. As soon as your genius adjusts itself to life, beautiful years will unfold before you, bringing you serious satisfaction and triumphant success.

You see, Madame, these comments on *Lélia* prove how I hasten to avail myself of the friendly privilege you permit me to enjoy. I confess that, listening to you yesterday, I felt proud to be allowed to call myself your friend. I was worried, though, by the consciousness of my own shortcomings. Hidden defects must be so easily apparent to a gaze as penetrating as yours. But I reassured myself with the reflection that your scrutiny would never detect in my attitude toward you anything other than sincere gratitude and the most zealous intention to be worthy of your regard.

SAINTE-BEUVE

Sunday morning

[We now turn from George Sand's new friendship with Sainte-Beuve to an older association of two years' standing.

The woman so warmly defended in the accompanying passage was the well-known tragic actress, Marie Dorval, who became George Sand's friend shortly after she took up her independent life in Paris.

Before George was known as an author she wrote a letter of admiration to Dorval and expressed a desire to meet her. On the very day of the letter the door of George's apartment was thrown open, while the vibrant voice which had thrilled her from the stage exclaimed, "Well, here I am!" Dorval then related that some time before her début on the stage she had written a similar letter to the actress Mademoiselle Mars, who received it without response. The memory of her own disappointment had been revived by George's hero-worship. Unwilling to wound her young admirer, she had rushed immediately to the address given in the letter.

This incident explains Dorval's character. She was generous to excess, always imposed upon by others, and recklessly exploiting her own strength. In acting, as in life, she was unable to conserve her forces, so that it sometimes happened that she played superbly until the end of the second act, when, having wasted her vitality, she would feel complete exhaustion and approach her great scene in a state of collapse. The next day the critics would score her for a mediocre performance.

After she lost her youth and beauty, Dorval was given unimportant rôles. When the public grew fickle, George Sand remained faithful and never refused help and solace when they were needed by her friend. For her first play, *Cosima,* George insisted on giving Dorval the leading rôle.

Toward the close of her life Dorval suffered from poverty, and even more from the selfish ingratitude of a daughter to whom she was devoted. Having given of herself too lavishly, she died, burnt out, before her time.

In her autobiography George Sand devotes an entire chapter to Marie Dorval. She seems always to have felt a profound sympathy for the woman whose sins of the flesh she found easier to forgive than cold-hearted selfishness and prudence. George could be bitter and cynical toward people who were mean or hypocritical, but an outgoing, self-defeating nature like Dorval's aroused her championship and compassion.]

GEORGE SAND'S DEFENSE OF MARIE DORVAL

1833.

Let me love her. I understand who and what she is. As for her faults, I know them. As for her vices—ah, that formidable word of yours! You are afraid of vice. And yet your life is saturated with it. You are unconscious of this truth or else you refuse to admit it.

Vice! How much attention do you give to it, you good people? Is it possible you do not realize that it is everywhere, around you and within you? Either your father is avaricious, or your mother tells lies, or your brothers are men without honor. Your father confessor has perhaps cheated at cards, or very likely your sister has sold herself, or your best friend has denied you ten times. You are not aware of these painful facts? How do you live, then, in such obliviousness? What do you do with your eyes, your ears and your memory? You call me a cynic, but I refuse to make a virtue of the sort of kindness which is only another name for blindness or hypocrisy. Those who indulge themselves in this false kindness are dupes and fools.

You say she has betrayed me. I am fully aware of it. But which of you, my good friends, has not done the same? She has betrayed me only once, and you have betrayed me time and again. She has repeated one thing I said to her in confidence, you have repeated as coming from me many things I never said at all.

[George Sand, on rereading this page fourteen years later, adds the following comment.]

1847.

This cynicism must have been due to disordered liver. But *she* remains the same and I shall always love her. Her soul is full of beauty. Her impulses are generous and tender, her intelligence is exceptional. She has wandered from the straight and narrow path and has suffered accordingly. And for that I love and respect you all the more, O Marie Dorval!

[Among George Sand's early souvenirs, the scrapbook next includes a vivid description of her emotional reaction to Beethoven. George Sand often declared that she loved music more than any other art. Technically she was not a musician, as her youthful playing of harp and piano was no more than a parlor accomplishment. But the possession of taste, sympathy and understanding made her a true musician in spirit and mind.

Maurice Dupin, her father, chose music as his profession and the violin as his instrument. He was playing with professionals and had even begun to compose, when the appeal of Napoleon caused him to forsake his musical studies for a military career. In the family home at Nohant George Sand hung her father's violin above the pillows of her bed. To the sound of this violin she had been born. It still hangs there, mute symbol of the father's renunciation of music and of the daughter's devoted love of what she always called the greatest of the arts.

The vision which came to George Sand while listening to Beethoven, reveals the sensitivity and imagination which gave to her emotions their intensity and to her writings their fame.

In this vision, she strongly identifies herself with Beethoven's conflict between celestial yearnings and earth-bound desires. The Beethoven conflict, revealed in his music, was also the essential drive of George Sand's life. She never ceased to struggle for the heaven of her dreams and never reached it. In old age she was resigned to unattainment.

The fact that toward the end of the vision she imagines herself as a darkened soul, shows her opinion of herself in comparison with others. Her sense of inferiority arose naturally from childhood identification with her plebeian mother, who was looked down upon by the aristocratic Dupin family.]

A VISION INSPIRED BY BEETHOVEN

April 6, 1833.

Here is a vision which came to me while the great symphony of Beethoven was being played.

I saw an immense plain, empty, monotonous. It was a heath, I think, an arid land without herds or men. I lay on the ground, broken with fatigue. At first I tried in vain to rise. Slowly I got to my knees, then found myself standing, face lifted to the sky.

Overhead the sky was somber. Fog was everywhere. Soon, in the distance, I saw yellow lights flicker from time to time, becoming each time more vivid, bigger. They continued to enlarge until they usurped the whole circle of the horizon. The sky turned orange yellow, then copper red. The more it took on this intense tone, the darker grew the plain, and the sharper the line of ground cut off at the horizon's edge, as one sees it in a sunset, only there was no sun in that world.

It seemed to me that by slow stages the sky came down until it hung over the earth like a palpable dome. I was about to touch it with my hands, I stretched out my hands.

But as I reached for the sky, the earth seemed to shrink back. I found myself left in the air, lost in the void and, I don't know by what miracle, balanced between heaven and earth.

Below me the ground grew steadily blacker, while the sky above was more illumined with hot and shining lights. I drew appreciably nearer to that luminous dome and was about to knock on the expanse of it when I became afraid. A great commotion took possession of the air, as if the burst of trumpets had split the element that carried me. I fell, I don't know where. I no longer knew myself. I no longer felt myself.

When I resumed my flight the sky was far away, the earth entirely plunged in shadow. The breath of a warm soft wind lifted me and I was borne on it for a long while, skimming above the plains, trying to find the way to heaven, but every few moments the wind dropped and let me fall back again. As I rose and fell I saw, across the horizon, long bars of gold piercing the dark clouds. I wended my flight in their direction.

The more rapidly I flew toward the illusive lights, the more steadily the horizon pulled back its vast boundary. Just as I thought to reach them the lights went out—to reappear farther on, veiled in immense obscurity. There was no end to the earth, and the sky kept beginning over. Strength went out of me. That journey seemed to last a century.

Finally the harmonious wind which stirred the ether swelled suddenly, and like an eagle, wings outspread, I mounted rapidly into the void. There was no longer anything above me nor below me save the ether.

I could see only dying fires of far-away worlds. I could hear distant echoes floating up from earth to the sound of a faint melody which, at every phrase, was cut off by the wind and scattered into eternity. Then all fell silent. I was alone, borne helplessly on the powerful drift of clouds.

From the depths of the air approached a confused noise of fluttering wings, drawing nearer and nearer. I saw coming, from different points of space, flocks of winged shadows which at first sight seemed to indicate the flight of migrating birds. Then, as I saw these beings distinctly, their aspect changed. But I would not know how to describe them, for as soon as I ceased to see them I lost all recollection of how they looked.

I know only that they came in long lines, like caravanseries of the desert, and that some of the groups were white and some were black. They came in such crowds and one so surged upon another that the air was dense with them and it was impossible for me to continue my effort to get through. I had to fly hither and thither in the midst of them. They, like me, were lost and troubled. They filled the night with thousands of plaintive or despairing cries.

It was a long-drawn anxiety, a turmoil of striving and fear. They were as helpless as gulls tempest-driven. Each of these souls was hunting the road to heaven, and yet not one of them knew or asked the way. Hurling themselves into space, they lost their companions. Those who were white as doves flew side by side with those who were black as ravens.

The wind grew wild and furious. Whole phalanxes of these winged creatures disappeared, falling like leaves of poplars in the breath of an autumn morning. I, and all the other wandering souls, could not make headway, and minute by minute we were pushed back toward the region of visible worlds. In vain we fought the celestial fury, in vain we asked that light be given and that hope might inspire us to find our way to the heights. Hope died as our strength waned, and those among us who had seemed transported toward the throne of God came tumbling back, rejected, to fall lower still.

A great voice dominated the tumult. I heard it clearly above the storm. "Forward," it cried, "fight on courageously. My tempest is rough but you are strong. My hand will lift you from the vortex. The peace you seek and all the blessedness of heaven are for the strong. The worlds below are the refuge of the weak."

The voice ended. The souls renewed their courage and redoubled their effort. Then came such terrible gusts of wind that my companions disappeared. I found myself alone in that immensity. Suddenly they returned and thronged the space where I was buffeted about by a contrary wind. Turn by turn, I was frightened by my aloneness or by the immeasurable number of drifting souls who, with me, encumbered the paths of eternity.

I noticed that those whose robes and wings were white ascended higher than the others, and I remembered that angels are white. It occurred to me to look at myself, and great was my dismay to see that I was as dark as if the smoke of the inferno had blackened me. Discouragement overwhelmed me. I folded my wings and let myself be tossed from space to space.

At last I fell exhausted to the bottom of I know not what nameless abyss. Shadows received me and enveloped me like a shroud.

A feeble ray came trembling through the fathomless blue of the abyss and, as from a dream, I awoke. Looking around, I saw frightful precipices opening before my feet. The narrow rock on which I was seated hung over a gulf out of which roared red-hot fire that seemed to come from souls aflame. Above me the sky, shut away by veils of night, seemed just across from the dangerous juts of rock.

Lifting my eyes toward the pale firmament, I saw a blue star trembling there, so feeble that every alternate moment I lost sight of it and thought I must have dreamed it. Gradually it became large, white and radiant, until its shining aureole poured toward me a flood of celestial light. Courage came back and I undertook my flight again. Ceaselessly from the yawning mouth of the abyss blew the same strident wind. It crowded me toward the bowels of the earth. At every new effort I fell back exhausted on the sharp rocks. My black wings clung bat-like to the jagged walls of the abyss. The lugubrious voice of that subterranean hurricane froze me with terror and anguish. Howling, it would rush into the gulf, then, shut within that sonorous prison, it would burst into infernal shrieks that seemed to shake the piled-up mountains.

That dreadful voice had nevertheless a grave solemnity which reassured me. Flames from the depths mounted toward me, red volcanic smoke choked me. The sides of the cliff ran with burning lava.

Suddenly came the sound of a trumpet. I knew it as the trumpet of the archangel, announcing Judgment Day. Like fragile crystal, my prison burst and fell in shreds around me. I discovered myself alone and free. This time I mounted rapidly and without effort toward the Lord of Hosts. Soft clouds, white as swan's down and golden as the sea at sunrise, spread themselves under me as I ascended into rarer, purer air. Languor laid hold of my senses. I floated like a swallow held up by the wind. Delicious tears rolled down my cheeks, fell upon my body, and carried away the black that had disfigured me. Little by little I became white as a lily. All around me were happy souls who lifted their hands and blessed the Lord. The gates of heaven swung wide, and I heard the voice of the Most High calling: "Come, all ye courageous, enter into my peace!"

But, after all, I saw nothing of heaven, for the symphony came to an end.

GEORGE SAND COMMENTS ON LÉLIA

[At this point George Sand inserted in her scrapbook a long analysis of *Lélia*.

Fragments of her reflections are given here, but the greater part have been omitted because *Lélia*, like other books of its kind, has lost its interest for the modern mind. It may be noted, however, that this careful analysis is an example of George Sand's capacity to plan and construct the novel she was preparing for the public. Evidently she did not always write instinctively, nor was she always pouring forth words under pressure of haste.]

February-April, 1833.

Lélia signifies disillusion, suffering, despair. Sténio expresses hope, confidence in the future, love.

In order to personify these two ideas it is necessary to explain how Lélia has lived; why, instead of being crushed, she has remained upright; why, instead of merging her destiny in that of the man who deceived her, she has decided to live out her own personal destiny, independent, isolated. Once it is understood how she was driven to accept the rôle for which she was not destined by society, one can pity her, but one is none the less chilled by her cynicism.

Sténio, to be made comprehensible, requires a counter biography. Why is he attracted to proud and skeptical Lélia, instead of loving a woman who is younger, more confiding and trusting, one who would obey rather than command?

Either the Lélia idea will descend toward the Sténio idea and recover faith through happiness, or else the Sténio idea will lose faith and be converted to skepticism. Then filial submission to the superior genius whose authority he cannot resist will absorb his destiny in that of Lélia.

In order to realize one of these two conceptions, and I prefer the second, it would be well to merge in wise proportions psychological analysis and narrative, but in any case the narrative should be merely the background or frame for analysis of character.

[While George Sand was hesitating whether to absorb Lélia in Sténio or Sténio in Lélia, she evidently tried out two imaginary letters from her hero to her heroine. These letters form no part of the novel. They appear to be experiments in Sténio's possible states of mind. Sténio might regard the heroine from one point of view or the other. The letters seem to have been composed for purposes of comparison and future decision.]

TWO LETTERS TO LELIA FROM STÉNIO

I
June 15, 1833.

If you did not love me it was because I was unworthy of you. Far from resenting your indifference, it has only increased my love. You have refused to lower yourself to my level. You have retained your superiority. I am humbled and vanquished. I accept the shame of this rôle, and from the abject depths into which I have fallen I lift toward you the secret inner voice of my purest desires.

STÉNIO

II

Lélia, your soul is as cold as a tombstone. You cannot understand my devotion because you are incapable of love. From the days of your youth, your heart has been as barren as it is to-day. You are afraid to accept my sacrifices because to you gratitude is a burden. Egoist! Egoist!

STÉNIO

[Of particular interest is George Sand's frank criticism of her own style.]

The style of *Lélia* is clear and excellent in the expression of feeling, that is to say, when it transcribes impressions and memories and when the words spring from the heart. It is sometimes obscure and confused when it tries to penetrate the depths of thought or to analyze ideas and follow out their consequences. It betrays lack of experience in exploring the secrets of the brain. At times it gives to truth the appearance of a paradox.

To remedy this defect in the pages already written, it ought to be enough to transfer certain phrases, change a dozen words here and there, and separate distinctly by visible signs, such as Roman numerals, the various digressions of thought. In the future it would be wiser to dwell on memories, rather than on ideas.

When it is a question of expressing abstract thoughts and of converting sorrow and despair into dialogues and arguments, it would be well to look ahead and plan, almost geographically, the succession of ideas.

But it is useless to think while writing, the thoughts and words will not find each other. Labor of the brain and that of literary execution must be done separately.

Then, too, the style would gain precision if, instead of dwelling on all the details, it omitted those of less importance or those which conflict and spoil the harmonious effect.

[The following quotation from *Lélia* serves to illustrate the style and feeling of the book.

The heroine is addressing her poet lover.]

"The emotions of the senses do not satisfy us: we want heaven and cannot find it. We seek for it in a being resembling ourselves. We spend on him the high energy which has been given us for a nobler use.

"Soon the veil falls, and behind the clouds of incense a human being is revealed in all his imperfections.

"Then we draw away from the illusion we have created. We are frightened. We are ashamed. We overthrow the idol and roll it in the dust.

"But because love is a necessity, we soon find ourselves seeking another idol. We crave love. And we deceive ourselves again and again.

"Finally the day comes when, disillusioned, wise, purified, we abandon all hope of finding lasting affection on earth, and lift toward God the homage we ought never to have given elsewhere.

"Love is not the violent attraction of all the faculties toward a created being. Love is the holy aspiration of the most ethereal part of the soul toward the unknown."

[In connection with her analysis of *Lélia,* George Sand inserted in her scrapbook a letter for François Rollinat, the friend to whom the book was largely addressed. François Rollinat was, according to Madame Karénine, "George Sand's alter ego." It is evident from their correspondence that George was accustomed to rely on him in the crises of her life. He lived conveniently near Nohant, at Châteauroux. Whether George returned from a journey, or from a love affair, made no difference to Rollinat. He was always ready and waiting to welcome her home with affectionate understanding.

The two friends were mentally congenial. For hours on end they enjoyed long discussions on ethics, religion, and the topics of the day. Each confided to the other all his troubles and, whether speaking or listening, each identified himself with the other to such an extent that it was difficult to tell where sympathy ended and self-condolence began.

"Rollinat," George wrote to Pierre Leroux, "is a saint and a martyr. He has been trying dull law suits since he was twenty years old, in order to provide for his father, mother, and eleven brothers and sisters. Not only does he slave for them, he wears his brothers' old shoes and cast-off clothes that they may be well dressed, while he goes about looking like a tramp.

"He detests his profession but will never abandon it so long as he feels this weight of family responsibility.

"And he has no love affairs, the good boy."

In the novel, Trenmor, who is Rollinat, is described as George Sand's ideal. In life she was always trying to be like Trenmor and failing in the attempt. Since Rollinat was her ideal man, one is left to wonder why George always fell in love with men who were his exact opposites. One is forced to conclude that mind and feeling were in conflict, and that she felt an irresistible attraction away from her ideal.

George Sand loved men who were selfish, weak and vain, although she liked and admired those who were strong and virtuous. She chose as friends noble burden bearers, and fell in love with clinging vines. In this perhaps she showed masculine greatness, since she followed an example set by many great men.

Other characters of the novel to whom George alludes in the following letter to Rollinat are Lélia, Sténio and Magnus.

The heroine, Lélia, is a cynical young woman. Like George Sand, she has suffered from an unhappy marriage and is in search of ideal love. She loses her heart to the poet Sténio, only to find that while her youth and beauty have caught his senses, he is oblivious to her spirit and mind. Wounded and disillusioned, she refuses herself to her lover and gives herself to God. Entering a convent, she becomes an abbess and devotes her life to humanity.

Sténio, after a degrading affair with a courtesan, turns again to his first love. But Lélia has put herself beyond his reach. In despair at his wasted life Sténio commits suicide.

Magnus, a monk, is also in love with Lélia. He is an infantile character, the slave of dogma and convention. His mind is in conflict between desire and conscience.

Trenmor is a philosopher. A large part of the novel is devoted to the dialogues of Trenmor and Lélia. They discuss the evils of their times and George Sand's suggested remedies. Her theories are commonplaces to-day, but they seemed heretical and sensational to the public of one hundred years ago. Trenmor and Lélia share the ideas of Susan B. Anthony and Carrie Chapman Catt in regard to the reforms necessary for women. They agree with Clarence Darrow about capital punishment, and with Judge Lindsey on prevention of crime and treatment of criminals.

On May 26, 1833, George Sand wrote to François Rollinat, "*Lélia* is an eternal conversation between us two."]

FROM GEORGE SAND TO FRANÇOIS ROLLINAT

You whose soul is strong and patient, whose head is cool and whose mind is full of the knowledge of good and evil; you who live laborious days resigned to obscurity—you stand to me as a symbol of virtue, you shine as a fixed star among fleeting meteors of the night.

You are man purified, man tested and proved, you are the new man of whom I dreamed when I described Trenmor.

By what association of ideas I proceeded from you to him, why I used so much fantasy and fiction in transforming you, the real man, into this imaginary character, why I altered the purity of my model by decorating him with puerile distinction and futile beauty of the body—all this I hope you may be able to divine— as for me, I remember nothing about it.

Perhaps, reading with your tranquil spirit what I have written with a soul preoccupied with its own misery, you will find in this labyrinth of imagination the magic thread which leads back to you.

I have lived so many lives, I no longer know in what classification of goodness or badness my own identity belongs. Some will claim I am Lélia, but others will remember that I used to be Sténio; I have lived through days of frightened devotion, passionate desire, violent combat and timid austerity, when I was Magnus. I may become Trenmor too. Magnus is my childhood, Sténio my youth, Lélia my maturity, and Trenmor will perhaps be my old age.

All these types are in me. All these moods of mind and heart I have possessed in varying degrees, following the course of years and the vicissitudes of life. Sténio is my credulity and inexperience, my rigorous piety, my fearful, eager waiting on the future, my deplorable weakness in that period of struggle which lies between youth and maturity. Indeed this resemblance has not been entirely outgrown. To this day I sometimes discover in myself the puerile grandiloquence and exaggerated candor of Sténio. But I express these qualities less and less, year by year.

Magnus, with his excessive needs, his sense of his own iron-clad destiny, and his eternal yearning for the impossible, represents another phase of suffering that I have combated and repressed. For a long time I was the victim of these forces within me. I still feel their instinctive efforts at reassertion.

Trenmor is the dream of philosophic serenity in which I have often cradled myself when fate has allowed me moments of relaxation in which to long for solace and peace.

At your side, my friend, I was Trenmor, I was you. Watching a great soul triumphant in adversity, I identified myself with your calm intelligence and hoped to achieve your real and lasting satisfactions. And you, listening to the recital of my incessant work, seeing the daily struggle between my reason and desires, you, in order to understand and share my suffering, became a man resembling me. You, Trenmor, became Lélia.

You could do this because, before overcoming, you also fought your way through the storms of life. You have felt those wounds of the spirit of which you are trying to heal me to-day. For many years you vacillated between a longing for your present serenity, and helpless yearnings toward the storms of the past. You have swung back and forth, as I have, between desires for suicide and the peace of the cloister.

And so, no doubt, we have both reflected these four different faces of life. Yet dare I say that I have ever been, that I can ever be Trenmor? How brief have been my hours of reason and of strength! How miserly God has been in withholding from me those consolations he has lavishly given you! I have let myself be consumed by a thirst for the unattainable which the powers of heaven have refused to quench.

[The following comment was added by George Sand on re-reading these notes thirteen years later.]

1846.

Of all this there is nothing left in my present me. I am merely the cypress above their graves. As for you, faithful friend, no one has ever been greater or better than you, François Rollinat.

PERSONAL RECOLLECTIONS, 1833

[The recollections which follow were written by George Sand after she had lived in Paris for two years. From the advanced position of her lately acquired independence she looks back with a sense of superior worldly wisdom at her former provincially-minded self. And in this retrospect her thoughts revert to the period of her marriage, when, as Madame Dudevant, she tried to forget personal unhappiness in service to suffering humanity.

In these memories she does not exaggerate the extent of her former devotion to others. Having learned something of medicine as it was practiced in those days, she grew her own herbs, compounded her remedies, and played the part of village doctor to ignorant peasants whose gratitude did not prevent them from gossiping about her behind her back. At one time Casimir Dudevant made frequent business trips, leaving her to manage the estate. The long, lonely rides she speaks of were taken to the neighboring village, La Châtre, whose social life failed to answer her insatiable yearnings for sympathetic companionship.]

I remember that I used to travel several miles to spend a dull evening with people who were duller still. Returning home on horseback I had to cover a couple of leagues, so that I would find myself alone on the road between midnight and two in the morning. They were almost the only hours of reverie and absolute solitude my work-limited life allowed me. They gave me an opportunity to think over my life, face my fate, and challenge my character. I fell into the habit of comparing myself with those by whom I was surrounded. It seemed to me that quite a distance separated me from them, and I wondered whether the same distance separated each of them from the others. Was this spiritual isolation which each possessed any proof of individual greatness? By no means. For there was one thing they all shared in common

—mediocrity. If anyone had an especial gift, it was meager and aborted.

This conclusion used to throw me into profound discouragement. Am I any better than these people? I asked myself. What have I done that they could not do better, if they so desired? The idealism that exalts me, the intensity that takes me unawares, my vague feeling about art and poetry, my religious effusions, my capacity for enthusiasm, the emotions that fill my heart and overflow on the most insignificant objects—what do these signify unless they are as C—— [Casimir Dudevant, her husband] says, the natural consequence of a bilious temperament predisposed to neuralgia?

Then I would say to myself, I fondly imagine I am different from my neighbors. I am more sensitive than one, more energetic than another. I have studied more than this one, I have lived more intensely than that one. I believe I am naturally religious and helpful, which most of them are not. They laugh at me for doing good, and I hope they are wrong. They tell me I am constantly deceived, yet I know I have found ineffable joy in good deeds. Nevertheless, in what does their supposed inferiority consist? I have a little more money than they, and I have an inner need for activity, a restlessness of soul.

They are poor, careless, or preoccupied with other duties—business affairs, domestic cares, bodily ills and I don't know what besides. Chance obstacles, about which they need not account to their consciences, imprison them within definite limits of prudence and personal interest. These limits I have broken down because I could. Moreover, the facility with which I give myself to others is not due to my own individuality, it is the result of the education I received. Had I been brought up like others, I should be like them. And anyhow, who knows? Perhaps their goodness is more effective than mine. With their cold reason, dry speeches, and unresponsive faces, they may know better than I do how to remedy the misfortunes of others. The soft-hearted are easily deceived. Perhaps the hard-hearted are just and discerning, while I, who wear myself out and waste my energies all day long, may in the evening turn away in sheer exhaustion from those who most need sympathy and help. My virtue is not great. My kindness is only feebleness, my devotion credulity. I have neither force nor penetration. How could I imagine myself endowed with a superior organization? Superior in what, pray tell?

When my reverie had reached this stage, I used to grow sad, and I remember melancholy autumn nights when I would see masses of thick clouds swirling above my head, veiling heaven from me while I searched in vain for the sight of a star that would reveal God's presence. Alas, I would cry, and is it thus that thou escapest me, O thou whom I pursue! God whom I serve, mystery I have embraced as reality, where art thou? Dost thou see me, hear me? I have done nothing that has persuaded men, or persuaded myself, of any real kindness in my vocation. Do I find favor in thy sight and dost thou watch over me as I walk through darkness alone? Am I thy disciple and thy child, or am I the victim of an illusion, without value or beauty? Am I a chosen soul, called by thee to accomplish some kindly mission on earth, or am I the prey of romantic fantasy, germinated in my poor brain like seed that has been carried by the wind and dropped no matter where?

What would I care for the world's approval if I felt close to God? But no answer, no word, no encouragement! What is life for? To what avail have I renounced the amusements and selfish idleness of the rich? Why do I ride on errands of mercy at night through boggy roads on a reeking horse? Why do I drag myself from comfortable warmth to drench myself in the icy mists of the morning? Why do I struggle against disgust, ennui, nausea and exhaustion at the bedside of strangers and ingrates? Why spend hours in filthy huts, cleaning the pus from sores?

They say pride of soul consoles me. What, pray, are the rewards of my pride? Is it not true that people hate me merely because I live differently from them? Those to whom I give alms in the daytime steal from me at night, those whom I nurse and console defame and insult me. Those who do not know me listen to the evil people say of me, and I am condemned without opportunity for self-defense.

I am the natural enemy of all who are different from me. And what comfort is there for my loneliness? Where is the friend who would do for me what I do for the first passer-by who comes knocking at my door? No, no, men are not my brothers. I can help and pity them. I cannot love them. I could love myself if thou didst speak to me, O God! If thou wouldst tell me that I am fulfilling a task imposed by thee, I could make myself walk through rough roads forever. I should die content, I would make no ambitious demands of heaven and eternity, if I had assurance that thy voice would say to me in my last hour, "My child, sleep in peace!" But we are so utterly abandoned here below. Nothing, not a sign, not one dream of heaven during my arduous nights; not a voice, not a phantom shape in the gloom through which I wander.

Then, overcome by despair, and feeling nearly mad, I would urge my horse into the blackness of night. Feeling the goad of the spur in his flank, he would bound ahead and begin to run, gripped by fear, ears and nostrils tense. Next I would shoot like an arrow through one of those great squalls which sweep over the plains, coming like a torrent from the horizon's edge. Taking a man by surprise, they whirl him around, or at least force him to retreat. Clinging to the neck of my horse I used to breast these winds, and he, feeling them cleave his chest, would quiver as if he had been struck by a whip, while whirlwinds of dry leaves crackled around us and beat in my face.

In the midst of these gusts of heavy warm wind, great white mists went floating by, blinding me for a second, making me feel faint. The young poplars that bordered the road bent, whistling, down to my head, and when I crossed a bridge the wind, imprisoned under its arches, boomed like thunder beneath my feet.

I loved those tempest noises, that wild flight, and the delirium that threatened to sweep me, or so I imagined, to the world's end. I would howl like a madwoman in the midst of the storm, "Here am I! Here am I! It is my turn to be judged!"

One place in my path was of sinister import for my family. It was at a bend of the road beyond the thirteenth poplar. My father, coming home one dark night, was thrown from his horse at that spot and killed. Sometimes I would pause there, recalling his memory, and in the light of the moon I would search the road for imaginary traces of his blood. But more often, as I drew near the place, I urged my horse forward at full speed. Giving him rein, I would dig my spurs into him just at the turn where the road dipped and made my course dangerous. I used to hope I could force the soul of my father to come forth from the invisible world. The danger I confronted was less great in reality than in my superstitious attitude of mind. I used to think that surely in this fatal place some mysterious sympathy would bring back all that remained of my father, if anything remained.

But in vain I summoned the feeble emanations the air might have preserved of that ardent spirit, as stormy, as susceptible to suffering as my own. In vain I held my breath, palpitating between hope and despair, and waited for him to call out, "Take care!"—a call that was ever in my ears as I rode across the shadow of the slim poplar. It seemed to me that from its foliage, or from the roots soaked in the same blood that flowed in my veins, would emerge the voice that was said to be so like mine. I waited for it, I summoned it, but I heard nothing but the sound of my horse's feet or the noise of the near-by waterfall. Too overwrought to content myself with reality, too enlightened to succumb to the charm of superstitious fancies, I would battle painfully with myself. If I acted in accord with the dreams of my mind, cold reason would confront me and defeat my dreams.

During all this period of my existence, as compensation for my everyday domestic heroism I would fall back on myself, scalpel in hand, and dig into my inner state, trying to discover the secret of my being and my destiny. Not until I had made myself suffer thoroughly would I stop, faint with fatigue of the spirit. Resuming my work among the peasants, I would try to find in bodily exhaustion the solace I needed for my soul.

I was unhappy—and virtuous. Still, there was in me some urge that devoured me. I ought to have been able to rid myself of its destructive force. Was it ambition? No, it was not that. To-day, when my ambition has reason to be satisfied, I am very well aware that there is still an ache in my soul, and I believe that even then I was aspiring toward something higher than the plaudits of the crowd. That which consumed me then, that which will consume me always, is the need of sympathy.

Tired of exciting myself without finding any close accord between myself and others, despairing of my work unless I could establish some communion between my soul and God, I next raised my cry of distress toward a world I did not know, a world that, as I imagined it, was full of glories and grandeurs. I idealized every celebrity. I knew how bad men are, I did not know how commonplace they are. I had seen the dregs of humanity swarming in the sun or languishing in prison. And also I had learned how self-centered, greedy, and insensitive are the privileged lords of earth. But I looked for intelligence among the intellectuals. I had faith in the world of art, culture, and eloquence. I was as naïve as a child about these things. Phrases from the books I read used to bring tears to my eyes. I would dream an ideal into every daub of paint, and when, in moods of melancholy, I declaimed classic literature to the walls of my room, I was so intense with feeling that my heart ached with the poetic suffering that I had made my own.

In this stage of experience I was convinced that on beyond the limitations of my life there existed an enlightened society where human beings endowed with the highest merit met to interchange the most exalted feelings and ideas. I had yet to learn that genius, whether it lives in a hermit's cell or spends itself outside, is always solitary, repressed, suffering, and misunderstood. I did not know then, as I now realize, that beautiful and noble people never group themselves about intellectual leaders, and that no moral hierarchy is ever accepted by men of talent.

Each one wants to be chief. Those who kow-tow and toady are liars and beggars, and yet for these same liars and beggars the masters compete with one another, watch one another, and hate one another!

My imagination was attracted to this world although it is the worst of all worlds. If anyone had told me that one day I should have access to it, there is one thing I should certainly have set myself to learn and that is spelling. I would have studied it whatever effort it cost. In those days I never doubted, although I feared, the immense superiority of the editor of the smallest sheet. I admired as poets all who wrote verses, and I would have walked ten leagues to see M. Balzac pass by.

These heights frightened me so that it never occurred to me to take a step toward them. I was content to say: Happy are those who have the right to some self-expression other than acts of mercy; happy are those who have at hand a pen with which to instruct or console. They do more good by one hour's inspiration than I can do in my whole workaday life. An idea set forth, a page of eloquence, may put the world forward a pace. If I can save the life and honor of a hundred obscure individuals, I shall die content, having accomplished all it is in me to do.

Life is like that, I told myself. And I went on.

This period of virtue and service was certainly not brilliant. And I suffered in it more than in any other phase of experience I ever lived through. Perhaps that is why I remember it with so much complacence. I love to recall that youthful spirit which the injustice of mankind and of fate had not yet been able to wither. For I was so self-depreciating that in all sincerity I used to compare myself with the brutes I saw vegetating around me, and in my foolish reveries I honestly believed them superior to me in many ways.

To-day I know that the highways of the world are paved with such brutes, so that one can't take a step without treading on one of them. I know just what they are worth, and I am more to be pitied than in the days when I was examining them under a magnifying glass, saying, "Maybe they are men, after all." At present my opinion is that it wasn't worth while to open one's eyes to examine them.

Great men—or those they call great—seemed to me in those days like giants. Poor young doctor that I was! I used to see so many human ruins that any biped who could walk on his feet seemed to me a fine individual. My mind was so affected by contact with the abject and deplorable that it is strange I did not go mad. I would have ended by believing that I also was a thief or leper if I had not escaped from those surroundings.

It is quite true that, in spite of all, I had moments of exaltation. Sometimes I would be passing a village garden, and behind its gay hedge I would see a family sitting in the rays of the setting sun: lovely children on the knees of a sturdy old laborer, a mother suckling a little one, a father coming home with his sheaf or his work tools over his shoulder. These people would be living, eating, laughing, under a roof that no longer leaked. And it was I who had repaired that house, I who had saved those children from smallpox, I who had prolonged the life of that grandfather with my rare old wine, I who had saved the son when, for lack of medical care, he was about to die in a furrow at harvest time.

I would go on farther and see a young man light a fire and carry his paralytic mother to her bed. I had saved him from conscription. Another would enter his hut alone and shut himself in with a mournful air. Because of his promise to me, he had not murdered his enemy on the way home—and as long as I lived he would not be a murderer.

I used to run away from the thanks of these people, but sometimes, after I had made a tour of the village, I would hide myself in the gloomy, solitary porch of the rustic church. Far off I would see an old woman kneeling at the entrance to the cemetery. She would be winding her distaff while she said a prayer for the dead. Behind the orchard and the moss-grown roofs of the village the moon would rise in the still red heavens. Then I used to cry, because my heart was full.

Was it pride? Perhaps. But God alone saw me, and that moment of softening and solitude was not too much to ask as recompense for such hard work done.

[Whenever George Sand stayed at Nohant she grew introspective and morbid, but as soon as she found herself back in her Paris apartment she forgot the old associations which led to bitter memories, and turned her attention to the present. She then lived fully, received fresh impressions, and made contact with people who were congenial.

Among her new acquaintances was the picturesque character, Hortense Allart. The letter written by this well-known woman to the suddenly famous but socially obscure George Sand was no doubt intended by her and accepted by George as exceedingly kind. Was not Madame Allart a member of the Gay family, so eminent in the literary circles of the day? Was she not a cousin of Delphine Gay, whose salon was a center of fashion? Madame Allart's place in the literary aristocracy of Paris was assured to her at birth, for she was the daughter of Mary Gay and the niece of Sophie Gay. These two, with Delphine, were known and noted under the collective title of "the authoresses Gay." The future was to find their writings as ephemeral and feminine as their title, but in the present they were popular and admired.

Madame Allart outshone her mother, her aunt, and her cousin. She was more than a novelist; she proved an amount of learning unusual in a woman by producing a series of works on history and philosophy. After achieving distinction as a *femme savante*, she added color to her reputation by writing her memoirs with a Rousseau-like frankness which was considered audacious.

Her love affairs were numerous and distinguished. Beginning with the elderly Chateaubriand, she had as lovers several other important men, including the angelic Sainte-Beuve. These affairs, conducted with discretion and talked about in whispers, were confessed by her to such friends as she felt were not censorious.

Madame Allart, therefore, was far more sophisticated than the George Sand of 1833, who at twenty-nine was still timid and doubtful of her powers, as is evident in the self-deprecatory tone of her reply to a letter which seemed to her precious enough to deserve a place in her scrapbook.

Several references in the accompanying correspondence relate to the society founded by Saint-Simon and continued at this period by his disciple Enfantin. The meetings of the society were largely attended by radicals, intellectuals, and all curious seekers after truth. Enfantin's teachings were a combination of new religion, old socialism, and the doctrines of Rousseau. He preached abolition of property, rehabilitation of the flesh, and equality of the sexes. So much stress was laid upon the importance of woman that, in the total absence of women's clubs, Saint-Simonism was the nearest approach to a suffrage society in Paris.

One would scarcely imagine, from reading George Sand's answer to Madame Allart, that in *Lélia* she had just completed an eloquent plea for the rights of woman, including higher education, property rights and divorce. It is interesting to observe that in this letter she refrains from any reference to the efforts made in *Lélia* to "ameliorate woman's fate."

The subjoined letters are plainly part of a preceding correspondence.]

FROM MADAME HORTENSE ALLART DE MÉRITENS TO GEORGE SAND

Norblay, July 26, 1833.

I admit that my first opinion of you was influenced by the gossip I heard about you. It was the sort of superficial judgment we all form of people we scarcely know. I did believe you were the sort of person you say you are. But I also believed that you were inclined to yield to passing influences, that you idealized the people who pleased you, and that you were inclined to grow enthusiastic over any man or woman who caught your imagination.

No, you do not seem to me to have limited ideas. I accuse you, rather, of clever inspirations; for instance, in *Indiana* you attack society, and in *Valentine* you yield to public taste. In proof of this, M. Planche has written a long article showing how *Valentine* conforms to the prejudices of conventional morality. Thus the bold views of your first novel are nicely smoothed over. I am intimately associated with many intellectuals, and I have noticed this characteristic in a number of them. Superior minds seem to follow their own inspiration, leaving carefully prepared plans to commonplace minds.

Your writing has a vigor, eloquence and force that no man of the present day can equal; yet the personality and sadness revealed in your books convinced me you were a woman.

The ancients established schools for the development of self-confidence and comradeship. They also encouraged the public appreciation of men of talent. Christianity destroys all this and leaves each one to work alone. Women fade away under the profound ennui which pervades their lives. Those of them who are ambitious grow weary of reading about life and looking on at life. Those who are capable of noble enthusiasms find no opportunity for expression.

I am counting on you to do something to ameliorate woman's fate. It is left to women to do this. I agree with you that we cannot defend the one-sided morality prescribed for women. But I do defend general morality, because without it no beauty would be left on earth.

The morality of women is really about the same as the morality of men. It is taught by nature. But the more enlightened one is, the more difficult and complicated morality becomes. It still remains the one true happiness.

This theme deserves to be developed further, but I shall not attempt it at present for fear of boring you. One part of your letter I did not quite understand. But I won't take up that matter unless you insist.

M. Béranger writes me that he is waiting with impatience for *Lélia*. The public is waiting also, and in spite of what you say I believe that the public knows what is worth while.

With kind regards,

M.

FROM GEORGE SAND TO HORTENSE ALLART DE MÉRITENS

July, 1833.

I find myself embarrassed by your comments. I care for your esteem, yet I cannot make up my mind to lie in order to keep it. You force me to admit that I have a great deal of egotism and a great deal of nonchalance. I realize that my indifference to Saint-Simonism has been criticized, and I doubt that criticism will alter my indifference.

As for *Indiana* and *Valentine*, I never thought of raising a question for or against society in either book. However much this disappoints you, it is true. Society is the last thing I care to condemn. Mankind delivered over to its instincts would not seem to me an improvement upon civilized man, even though the latter is far from perfection. And anyhow, what can I do about it? I am exceedingly feminine in my ignorance, inconsequence of ideas, and lack of logic. You have said it exactly—I lack accuracy and sequence. Do please understand this is not superiority, it is the infirmity of a passive nature that has been crippled. I have not studied anything and I do not know anything, not even my own language. My mind is so lacking in precision that I never could learn the simplest rule of arithmetic. Do you think that a mind like mine could be useful to anybody, or any cause? In spite of our affinity, you are greatly my superior in energy, reason, intelligence and knowledge. I have nothing but sensations. I have no will to achieve. For what, for whom, should I achieve? Beyond two or three people, the outside world does not exist for me. You see I am good for nothing. But you, both by nature and by gifts, are good for everything. You need no assistance from me. Have compassion for my social uselessness and let me keep your kindly thought and friendship.

The way you have of driving people, Madame, should be directed to great and strong souls. Mine is not one of them, although I admire them. It is the mission of powerful natures to pity and comfort those who are weaker. Work for the welfare of women in general and extend to me in particular your kindness and tolerance.

Good-by, Madame. Are you coming back soon?

I am cordially yours,

G. S.

TRANSLATION

THE dawn is here. Come, angel of the morning, the dew is falling and you will feel the penetrating cold. Have you no fear of cold nor of clinging mist? Come, the windows are open. My room is prepared for you with flowers. I am waiting for you.

It is the hour for slumber. If you do not come soon, I shall fall asleep.

At last you are here! Blessed art thou, son of heaven, give me thy forehead to kiss, let thy black hair fall over me, thy gorgeous hair a cubit long!

Oh, but an angel with floating hair is beautiful in the morning! Why is it that men do not have long floating hair?

Come, nameless one, sit at my bedside. You speak no language, you do not try to reveal yourself in words. That is why I love you, that is why I understand you so well.

Silent angel, put your cool hand on my shoulder. No man has ever touched it with his lips.

What flowers are those upon your forehead? Unknown flowers, flowers more beautiful than any woman has ever worn. Their perfumes are intoxicating, my angel, shower them upon me, tear the leaves from your dewy crown and strew them over me.

It is enough. I am dying. I want to live for another dawn in which to see you again. Adieu, the light breaks. Go quickly, my treasure, so that no one will see you, for they would steal you from me and then I should have to give my love to men.

Adieu, let me kiss your snowy neck and your forehead where shines a star. Give me a feather from your wing, that I may keep it as proof that you have been with me. It will be a souvenir of happiness.

Why do not men have wings with which to come at night and fly away in the morning?

I prefer thistledown to a man. You blow on it and it is lost in the air. Man never sublimates himself and never dissolves into spirit.

Go now, angel of the morning. I am falling asleep; kiss me on my forehead and make my soul as beautiful as yours.

MADAME DUPIN'S RECOLLECTIONS
OF ROUSSEAU

[The accompanying fragment has no personal bearing upon George Sand except as it reveals her cherished memories of the stern, aristocratic grandmother with whom she lived as a child.

The *Confessions* of Jean-Jacques Rousseau contain the well known story in which he accuses himself of having stolen three pounds ten from M. Dupin de Francueil, who was George Sand's paternal grandfather. This confession of theft having become an anecdotal classic of French literature, George Sand here incorporates her grandmother's notes and reminiscences on the subject. For a brief period Jean-Jacques acted as secretary to M. Dupin.]

"Francueil once said to Jean-Jacques—'Shall we go to the Théâtre Français?' 'Why not?' replied Rousseau. 'It won't hurt us to yawn for an hour or two.' Probably that was the only witticism Jean-Jacques ever attempted in all his life, and it cannot be considered very witty. Perhaps it was on that same evening that Jean-Jacques stole his celebrated three pounds ten from Francueil.

How fatuous it was of Jean-Jacques to confess that alleged swindle! Francueil himself had no recollection of being robbed. He believed that Jean-Jacques invented the theft in order to exhibit the exquisite susceptibility of his conscience. Good old Jean-Jacques, to-day you would have to crack your whip a little louder to make us even prick up our ears." (Taken from the notes of my grandmother.)

My grandmother, Aurore de Saxe, often told me about her first meeting with Rousseau. At that time he lived like a hermit, a prey to the morbid misanthropy which was so ridiculed by his idle and frivolous friends.

Mademoiselle de Saxe, widow of Comte de Horn, who was a son

of Louis XV, had just married M. Dupin de Francueil, a charming man of the world, whose only contribution to the literary history of the eighteenth century was made through his intimacy with Jean-Jacques and his intrigue with Madame d'Épinay.

After marriage, Madame de Francueil persistently begged her husband to make her acquainted with Jean-Jacques. Before her wish was gratified, *La Nouvelle Héloïse* was published, and Madame de Francueil devoured it in one gulp, as she herself said, forgetting, like the court lady of whom Jean-Jacques speaks, both the ball for which she was dressed and the carriage waiting for her at her door.

The enthusiasm excited by the heroine, Julie, increased her desire to see the author, and Francueil went in search of the "sublime bear," as he was called in the inner circle.

The sublime bear arrives, looking half silly, half surly. He allows himself to be led into the parlor, where, instead of politely asking for the mistress of the house, he seats himself in a corner without speaking to anyone. In short, he yields with very poor grace to the curiosity of this lady about whose age and personality he has not even been interested enough to inquire. She on her part dawdles over her toilet, unaware that the recluse has been brought into her house and that she has only to take a step to see the great man. Francueil, by way of adding a finishing touch to his surprise, has not had the visitor announced. Leisurely, in the lady's boudoir, the long flowing locks are dusted with blond powder, the robe of damask satin, striped with blue and silver, is slipped over the head and spread out over three hoops. At last the toilet is completed. My grandmother at twenty-five was as beautiful as an angel—she still was at seventy-six, when she lay dead in her coffin, her lace cap on her head, her white shroud draped about her, and her face as noble as the soul that had animated the beautiful body.

Entering the drawing-room she saw a small, badly dressed, frowning man who rose clumsily and stammered a few awkward words.

Jean-Jacques had been described to her so often that she recognized him at once. She tried to speak, but burst into tears. And Jean-Jacques, overwhelmed by such a reception, tried to thank her—and burst into tears himself. Francueil, in an effort to hearten them, tried to joke, but he also felt his tears overflow. The three then hastened to the dinner table, so that all this weeping might be controlled. But Madame de Francueil could not eat. Francueil lost his wits, and Jean-Jacques slipped away, leaving the table without having said a word. Perhaps he was dissatisfied because his reception was an emphatic denial of his pretension that he was the most persecuted, the most hated, and the most calumniated man on earth.

[The brief item appended below indicates that George Sand's financial worries were sometimes met by good resolutions which, as is a matter of common knowledge, she was far too open-handed to keep.]

The first of October, 1835. Definite beginning of retrenchment.

Solid, fundamental establishment of public and private order in my finances for the months of October and November:

Owe........ 6,000.   Possess........ 0

GEORGE SAND TO THE EDITOR OF THE "INDRE JOURNAL"

September 9, 1835.

DEAR SIR:

In your columns an oracle, whose signature does not betray his identity, brutally attacks the morality of my books. I willingly leave to the critic all my defects and all my deficiencies of logic. But in this province of Indre, which is my adopted country, I forbid any sycophant of social abuses to select me for his holocaust when he is pleased to offer homage to the powers he wants to placate, whether the reward he seeks is to make himself a name in default of talent, or to obtain the protection of that world which so frequently pays for words in default of deeds.

A few weeks ago one of our gifted men said, "It is discouraging to write for people who do not know how to read." I know a sadder fate. It is writing for people who do not *want* to read. No journalist can divine an author's thought by merely looking at the color of the cover of a book. The public is aware of this. It is to the public I appeal in challenging the interpretations of the chaste critic who pretends to explain the purpose of all my works, and I here and now affirm that this enlightened judge of *Indiana* and *Valentine* and *Lélia* and *Jacques* has neither understood nor read one of these books.

If the candor of this accusation wounds him, since my sex does not permit me to challenge him nor him to challenge me, I constitute as my defender any compatriot of mine who, as a man of honor, is willing to give and receive satisfaction.

Allow me to remain, etc.,

GEORGE SAND.

[George Sand is now thirty-three years old. She has changed tremendously from the woman of twenty-nine who composed most of these *Sketches and Hints*. She has passed through her great love affair and has outlived her romanticism and individualism. Less emotional and more mental, she is entering the period of serious maturity.

Félicité de la Mennais, to whom the following letter is addressed, was a poet, an orator, and one of the great writers of his century. Born of a rich family of shipbuilders who had been ruined by the Revolution, he entered the priesthood, where he became a noted defender of the established order as exemplified in the two dominant forces of his day, Catholicism and monarchism.

The orthodox priest seemed destined to a successful career in the church. For his services as champion of the papacy he was about to be made a cardinal, when gradually he grew unorthodox and began to proclaim his own ideas instead of the doctrines of the church. Twice he was summoned to Rome to explain his writings. Twice he was sentenced to deny publicly his opinions. When he reached the age of fifty he was excommunicated for writing *Paroles d'un Croyant*. This book went into almost one hundred editions and was translated into every language in Europe.

The heretical priest, believing himself a true Christian, refused to accept the church's ban. He continued to hold mass, and the people who loved him continued to attend his church. Finally, as ultimate punishment, he was anathematized. The church's curse frightened his followers away, and separated the unfortunate man from his family and friends. He became a martyr to his convictions and endured poverty, hatred and misunderstanding. Forced to begin a new life, he turned radical. The former defender of monarchism became an active republican; the champion of papacy emerged as a Christian socialist. As a republican he changed his name from de la Mennais to Lamennais, and as a socialist he defended the cause of labor as brilliantly as he had once championed the supremacy of the pope. It was at this stage of his career that Lamennais founded the magazine *Le Monde*, which was established to promote freedom of conscience and all liberal ideas.

When George Sand met Lamennais he was already a renegade and had published his first sensational book. She had paid a glowing tribute to *Paroles d'un Croyant* in her third *Lettre d'un Voyageur*, written while she was in Venice. This appreciation was the beginning of the sympathy which existed between them. Two years later, when she was introduced to Lamennais by Liszt, who was his ardent disciple, she felt slightly disappointed in her ideal leader of radical thought. "He has more of the priest in him than I supposed," was her first impression. She expressed herself as ready to defer to him so long as he was not dogmatic. "But I reserve my right to a certain liberty of conscience," she wrote to Madame d'Agoult.

While she was at Majorca and in need of money, George sent several generous contributions to Lamennais. On one occasion she gave him two thousand five hundred francs to help establish his magazine. In accepting the invitation of Lamennais to write for him, George still further sacrificed money to conviction, and also brought down on her head the contumely of her friends, who considered Lamennais a fanatic. They knew that for lack of capital *Le Monde* could not long survive, and they were reluctant to see her injure her reputation by linking her work with that of an unsound visionary. But George, always heedless of reputation, chose to follow her sympathies. Although she saw the dangers of association with Lamennais, she knew that her popularity would increase the subscription list of his unpopular magazine, and she could not resist the temptation to help the underdog.

At the instigation of the editor, she undertook to attract the interest of women readers by writing a series of letters to an imaginary woman named Marcie. But Marcie soon became so real to George that she tried to convert her to feminism and divorce. With her usual faith in those she loved and admired, she could not foresee that an ex-priest, turned radical but remaining a bachelor, might fail to appreciate the reasons for divorce and the need of feminism.

In judging George Sand's attitude toward the men by whom she was surrounded, it must be borne in mind that she never received any training deserving the name of education. While boys

of her age were taken into the French school system, which prepared them for higher education, she was put in charge of an
elderly tutor left over from the previous generation, the tutor
of her father. While these boys were taught the classics in college,
she spent three years in a convent, where her keen intelligence lay
dormant. At eighteen she married and allowed her mind to be
devastated by domesticity. In the meantime young men who were
later on to become her friends were receiving the training necessary to enter the arts and professions.

What wonder that she was unduly impressed by the mental
equipment of her friends and painfully humble about her own
ignorance? And in an age when accomplishments were considered
more appropriate for women than intellectual pursuits, what was
more natural than the superior attitude of the men who were
her friends?

When she responded to the pressure of outside opinion she felt
convicted of inferiority, but when she listened to her own inner
promptings she felt also the power of her mind. The following
letter to Lamennais indicates her habit of swinging back and forth
between these two influences.

The letter commences in her best feminine apologetic manner.
But as the flow of language continues she is carried away by her
subject, and grows self-assertive with the certainty that she is
right. Soon she knows more than her master. This contradiction
of feminine subserviency and mental arrogance is characteristic
of her. It is not, as many have believed, an indication of insin-
cerity, but rather it demonstrates the difficulty she experienced in
adjusting herself to an environment which, if not always inimical,
was at least wholly unprepared for a woman as intellectual as the
uneducated George Sand.]

GEORGE SAND TO THE ABBÉ DE LAMENNAIS

February 28, 1837.

DEAR SIR AND EXCELLENT FRIEND:

When you persuaded me to undertake this work, you did not
know you were leading me to the uncertain ground where I now
stand.

When I began the *Lettres à Marcie* I intended to write them in lighter vein. But the appeal of the subject is serious, and my mind has been carried along by a force that is like an invincible will. This frightens me, for on the few occasions when it has been my privilege to listen to you with the respect and veneration you inspire, I never thought to ask for your opinions on the present condition of women. Your mind is so occupied with religious and political questions that you may not be interested in this question with which I am struggling to-day.

Strange as it may seem, although I have written on this subject throughout my entire literary life, I scarcely know on what to rely in my own search for truth. I have never summed up my ideas and impressions, and in the past I have reached rather indefinite conclusions. Nor can I deny that my present definite conclusion is derived from inspiration alone. I do not know whence my conviction came nor whether it is mistaken, I only know that I find within myself an inescapable certainty which may be the voice of truth and may be merely the impertinent voice of pride.

However, now that the subject is launched, I greatly desire to continue the *Lettres à Marcie* as long as I can use them for the discussion of questions relating to women. I should like to write about marriage, motherhood, etc. But in some instances I fear that my natural intensity may carry me farther than you would approve. Perhaps it would be advisable to consult you beforehand. But can I pause at every page to ask for your instruction, and can you take time to fill in the gaps left by my ignorance? Certainly not, since the paper must go regularly to press.

As for me, I have a thousand things to attend to all day long. When evening comes and I can devote an hour to *Marcie*, it would be futile to use that hour in the search for enlightenment. I must produce.

Anyhow, I doubt that study and reflection would help me

much. Each time (I had better say on the few occasions when) a good idea occurs to me, it comes suddenly when I least expect it. So what can I do? Shall I feel free to follow my own impulsions? Or must I beg you to look over every manuscript I send to the paper? Such an arrangement has many drawbacks. A corrected page loses its unity. Corrections rob a manuscript of its logic and help to destroy its harmony. Often it happens that a house remains standing as long as it is left untouched, but as soon as repairs are begun on a corner of the wall, the whole house topples over.

To obviate these difficulties, suppose we agree on two things; first I shall confess the leading ideas I wish to advocate, then you will authorize me to write freely without bothering you about details. I don't know to what extent the public will hold you responsible for my ideas, but I believe you care very little for public praise or blame. However, my affection for you is so great and my confidence in you so unquestioning, that even if I were certain of being in the right I think I would yield to your judgment rather than lose your approbation.

Let me tell you briefly my boldest idea. I believe we should ask for a law which would grant the right of divorce in marriage.

I can find but one remedy for the barbarous injustice and endless misery of a hopelessly unhappy marriage. That remedy is the right to dissolve such a marriage with liberty to marry again.

I am not of the opinion that divorce should be granted lightly, nor for lesser reasons than those for which legal separation is allowed to-day. Nor am I pleading for myself. As far as I am concerned I would rather spend the rest of my life in prison than marry again. But there are others who need a divorce law. There are men and women whose affection for each other is so enduring and imperious that it cannot be suppressed. Indeed I see nothing in the old civil law [which denied the right of divorce] that can curb or crush such affection. And looking toward the future it must be conceded that the old law will be less and less effective in suppressing strong affection, because as human beings progress, their love will become more worthy of enduring interest and mutual intensity, so that the power of love will increase in proportion to the development of intelligence.

It is true that in the past social stability has suffered from uncontrolled passions which were the result of vice and corruption. Such passions have always existed and no law has ever been strong enough to check them. It is not for their sake that we demand a changed law. The increasing need for a divorce law arises from the higher order of attraction between the sexes.

Strong characters, great souls animated by faith and goodness, are sometimes dominated by passion which seems to come from heaven itself. What can be said of such examples? And how can one write about women without discussing a question which takes the most important place in their lives?

Believe me I know this one subject better than you do. And for once the disciple summons courage to say: Master, in this direction there are paths you have not trod, abysses whose depths you have not seen. You have dwelt with angels. I have lived with men and women. I know how people suffer and why they sin. I know how much they need a law which would make virtue possible. Please trust me. No one would work for this law with more respect for virtue and with less thought of self. For I shall never try to extenuate my past errors, and my present age enables me to look on calmly at the emotional storms that die down and disappear on my horizon.

Send me a word in answer. If you forbid me to continue, I will stop the *Lettres à Marcie* where they are. I will do whatever you command. For there are certain points on which I am willing to remain silent, and I do not imagine that I am called upon to make the world over.

Good-by, father and friend, no one loves and respects you more than I do.

[After George's services on *Le Monde* had been discontinued, the unfrocked priest, whom George persisted in calling the Abbé, indulged in sharp, rebuking criticisms of his former collaborator. In one letter to Marcie, George had commented on the fact that "men forget the apostles and violate their teachings until they reach St. Paul's imperious principle of the subjection of women, then with extraordinary ardor they insist that every law based on this principle must be obeyed." These sentiments published in his magazine must have been intolerable to Lamennais, who in his *Criticisms and Thoughts* proclaimed himself the enemy of woman's emancipation, and gave it as his opinion that women should obey their husbands and submit themselves to men.

After their estrangement George, as though unconscious of his animosity, continued her reverential attitude toward "the Abbé," and never said anything more severe about him than that "he did not seem to understand the mission of woman."

Jules Janin, whose words of appreciation were cherished by George Sand in her scrapbook, was a distinguished critic of drama and literature. Even to-day a woman receiving a similar tribute of friendship from such a lovable, large-hearted man would be likely to preserve it, as George did, to reread in moods of discouragement. How much more generous it was, then, from a man to a woman some ninety years ago! Jules Janin, in this letter to George Sand, seems almost to have succeeded in treating her as an equal.

But his superior manner begins to appear as he stresses her need of authority. It is plainly in evidence as he invites her to join his staff, where she is to do her best work advised by the guide he has wisely selected. Again he betrays his certainty that she is, in some special sense, in need of guidance, when he warns her not to follow her own genius because it leads her astray—that is, away from his opinions. But when he wants her to come on his magazine he forgets his former warning and urges, "Let your own genius advise you."

This desire to dictate and dominate was present in many of George's friends. The exceptions were the men of greatest stature. Liszt, Balzac, Flaubert, and Prince Napoleon were among those who accepted her as she was. Musset, Michel, Chopin, and these two men, Lamennais and Janin, were among those who wanted her to conform to their traditions. True, their will to dominate was mixed with love and admiration, but that made it more difficult to withstand.

George Sand's happiness, as she often explained, was found in her friends, and her friends were, with few exceptions, men. Naturally she did not want to antagonize and lose them, so there developed in her a placating attitude which was often irritating, sometimes pathetic, and at other times absurd. Her artist friends were regarded by her as great and wonderful, their works were masterpieces. Her own books she called pot-boilers, and herself she called commonplace. Her conscious self was sincerely self-depreciating. But from the unconscious welled up a blinding force which gave to her convictions and opinions the courage and confidence of a Deborah.

The occasion of this letter from Jules Janin was a request from George Sand for an article in praise of the Italian engraver, Luigi Calamatta, who was living in extreme poverty. She had suggested a comparison of Calamatta's work with the art of Ingres. Her own article, *Ingres and Calamatta,* was prepared for *Le Monde.* She then set herself to get other appreciations from influential critics and succeeded admirably, as the praise instigated by her and signed by well-known names appeared in several magazines. As a result the young artist, whose work had been unnoticed, won speedy recognition.

Referring to *Ingres and Calamatta* Madame Karénine says, "It was the first of an endless series of articles, letters, notices and prefaces from the pen of George Sand. It is another example of the generous effort which George Sand exerted, as long as she lived, in behalf of the friends, acquaintances, or even strangers who needed aid and protection. During her entire career she never refused her services to help create recognition for a new author or unknown artist. Sometimes she simply recommended to the public a book or painting that had just appeared."]

JULES JANIN TO GEORGE SAND

February 18, 1837.

MADAME GEORGE SAND, LA CHÂTRE (INDRE):

Surely you must realize that your slightest desires are accepted by me as commands. Even though you had not appealed to me in behalf of Calamatta, I should have remembered your concern for him. If his masterpiece were unrecognized by others it would still be appreciated by me. But since you are so keenly interested in the man and his work, you can do more for him than I can. You understand—no one better understands—the pure art of Raphael of which M. Ingres is, so to speak, the original imitator. Why, then, do you turn to a less initiated writer? Why ask an outsider to proclaim your ideal? You have, thank God, an all-powerful pen. Write the article yourself. Praise M. Calamatta as much as you like. Your appreciation, exactly as it is written, will be printed in the *Journal des Débats*, which loves you as a noble child gone astray.

Do you remember the day you came to see me in a mood even more discouraged than usual? I gave you some good advice which you have not followed. I told you that, to attain its fullest development, your great mind needed one thing it has always lacked—authority.

As long as you refuse to accept any definite guidance, you, and the world at large, will never know your true worth. Very likely you will die without having realized the tremendous secret of the power and endowment which agitate your being.

That day at my house I recommended to you as guide and mentor the noblest, most intelligent, most tolerant mind of our day, M. Bertin senior. He is the best equipped man I know. He was chief adviser to M. de Chateaubriand, whose manuscripts *Les Martyrs, Atala,* and *René* were corrected by M. Bertin. In him are preserved all the best traditions of the eighteenth century.

You could not ask for a better teacher, you whose need of a teacher is so great.

But no, you are so tenacious of personal liberty you will not listen to prudent and disinterested advice, at least you will not listen very long. You seem to find happiness in following your own enthusiasms without definite aim or plan. You jump into the saddle with the first wild idea of revolt which meets you on the road and ride with it until you both fall into the ditch. Poor great mind that you are, you wish to be absolute master of yourself. You cannot see that in refusing submission to ennobling discipline you often yield obedience to minds unworthy of comparison with your own.

If during the last few years you had been led by a guide who was true, devoted but inflexible, if you had had at your side an intelligent mind to advise, encourage and applaud you, where might you not be to-day!

But you have rebelled against salutary obedience, and while so doing you have bowed your head beneath the yoke of a man who has exploited you as a peasant cultivates a field. I refer to your present editor [Buloz] of whom you have a right to complain. He has taken advantage of you in every way. You who are so good, you who refrain from harming others, have been entangled by this man in all his hatreds, blunders and stupidities. He has treated you as though you were a newspaper, a book, or even a binding. He has made of you anything he could use, and as far as he was able he has compromised you in his own political and literary villainies.

You tell me that your books are going slowly. It is not surprising when one considers the kind of promoter you have. This is literary justice, of all justices the most unjust. Don't you see that your works are buried under the universal anathema directed toward that barterer of books? Don't you see that you yourself are treated without mercy because of your association with him?

That man, in his magazine, has the habit of abusing all books which he is not allowed to convert into merchandise. When, therefore, he offers his goods for sale, those who would not willingly do you an injury are nevertheless determined to injure him. Authors whom he has attacked need something more than virtue, they need to possess talent superior to your own in order to rise above their wounded feelings. If *Indiana* were not *Indiana*, if *Valentine* were not *Valentine!* When, therefore, his merchandise is signed George Sand, all that your friends can do is to remain silent. That explains why the announcement of an edition of your works, which is a great literary event, has met with so little response from the public. I who am so attached to you, I who consider you a master, would before this have written of George Sand in my *Journal*, had I not been afraid of helping your exploiter. This is sad to confess, but it is the truth.

Whence I conclude that this time you are right, you ought to break away from that man. It is a shame and a pity to be associated with him.

I was so moved by the few words you wrote that if I had had a thousand francs I would have sent them to you on the instant. You ought not to need money in the midst of such riches as are yours. Financial worries must not be added to your other burdens. Since that man leaves you stranded, we are going to find a way to snatch you from his clutches. I know some booksellers who might suit you. I have already spoken of this matter to Maurice Schlesinger, a capable man and a past master in the art of success. He seems willing to become your publisher, in which case I would gladly correct your proofs and your mind could be at rest. Therefore, send us information in regard to your books which have been published, those not yet published, what you owe this man, what he will give you in return, and the amount of money you need. Trust me completely. I shall do better for you than for myself.

And now to return to my first point. I take pleasure in informing you that the *Journal des Débats* is doubling its format. If you are willing to write for us, you shall have ample space. Contributions from George Sand, in which her opinions would not be compromised but where her talent would shine in all its brilliancy and distinction, would, I think, be received with enthusiasm. When you consider the success you have had in the *Deux Mondes,* in spite of its limited circulation, you can imagine what success would be yours in the *Journal des Débats*. How I should like to see you with us, advised by Bertin and accepted by our admiring public. You may protest in vain. There alone will you find the opportunity worthy of you. There is your future, and in that future you will find peace, calm, repose, everything you have missed. Let your own genius advise you!

I have read with pain your first article in collaboration with M. de la Mennais. M. de la Mennais has a noble mind but he is unbalanced. His fads and fancies may help to sustain him and keep him alive, but they are fatal to his associates. How many talented young men have been led astray because they chose to follow him! Where will he lead you? To what destination, or rather to what abyss? How can you consent to be connected with a publication for which he receives all the honor and which will inevitably cease with him? Why do you let yourself be influenced by his wild ideas? You see how much I love you. I am seriously concerned for you. Then, too, I take pleasure in scolding you. Your letter is so kind and friendly, yet so lacking in the enthusiasm with which you usually write to your friends, that this is the only way I can answer you.

Good-by. I have been trying to negotiate the purchase of a puppy. Its father and mother are very fine animals and they have promised me to get to work on the earliest possible day. Anais is well, and so are the children. Much love from us both.

J. JANIN

GEORGE SAND TO JULES JANIN

It was good of you to answer me so promptly and conscientiously, dear comrade. Many thanks for the kindness of your attitude toward Calamatta. But before I received your letter I had sent my poor effort to the *Monde*. I cannot recall it, nor can I write another article, as I really am stupid in work of this kind.

Also it simply isn't in me to work for the *Débats*. Opinions are sacred things, even for a woman. But leaving aside matters of opinion and considering the question solely from the literary standpoint, please realize that I have none of the qualifications for journalism. I haven't the faintest shadow of wit. I am heavy, prolix and declamatory. The stuff I am writing for the *Monde* would not please the *Débats*, and the ideas I express would probably not be accepted. My friend, how can you expect anyone else to amount to much in the magazine you write for? How can you ask anyone to risk his reputation in a realm where you are incontestably supreme? I shall never attempt to rival anyone. I am too apathetic for that. And to enter into competition with a sovereign would suit me still less. I do not feel I have the strength to contend with an established reputation. Who knows whether that fame of yours, which I acclaim to-day with such pleasure and affection, would not seem to me unbearable as soon as I felt it crush me! No, I am happier as I am. Let me stay in my corner. Besides, I solemnly declare to you that I am not ambitious for money or reputation. I have written what I could, and now all I long for is rest. I would like to hang up my pen beside my pipe.

I am not on the staff of the *Monde*. I do not collaborate with anyone. The title of collaborator with Abbé de Lamennais is an honor which will never fit me. I am his devoted servant. He is so good and I love him so much that I would give him as many ounces of my blood and my ink as he asked of me. But he will not demand much because he doesn't need me, for which the Lord be praised. I am not vain enough to believe I am helping him, except as my slight contributions obtain a few more subscribers to his newspaper, which paper will last as long as it can and remunerate me as it can. I am not worrying about that. Abbé de Lamennais will always be Abbé de Lamennais. And no amount of advice, guidance or collaboration will ever make of George anything but an average sort of fellow.

I do not doubt the kindness and the wisdom of M. Bertin, but there is really no reason why I should beg for any special help from him. My kind of work would not suit him. Besides, now that my hair is growing gray, my mind is somewhat set in its own ways, so that it would be difficult for me to acquire the grace, conciseness, and other qualities necessary to please his readers. Believe me, it is better to let each one abide by his own limitations. "It is ambition that ruins men. Let us not force our talent. We must offer the public only the work in which we excel." You see I have been reading Sancho Panza and his thirty thousand proverbs.

My sole desire at present is centered on one thing—to sell the work I have done so that I won't have to face any more work in the future. You can't imagine, my friend, the disgust with which literature inspires me at present. (My own, I mean.) I am passionately fond of the country, and, like you, I enjoy everything that belongs to family and home; dogs, cats and, above all else, children. I am no longer young. I need to sleep at night and take things easy through the day. Help me to extricate myself from the paws of Buloz and I shall bless you as long as I live, and I shall write you manuscripts with which to light your pipe. I will raise greyhounds and Angora cats for you, and if you will give me your little daughter to care for, I will send her back to you healthy, beautiful—and naughty as the devil, because I shall spoil her most awfully. Great heavens, you ought to understand all this, you who are so good, so simple, so unaffected in your ways, you who are yourself so little of a wit and so unlike all other critics. You have endured success more than you have sought it.

It has been great, but had it been merely mediocre you would have accepted it with that fine indifference I love so well. Do you know what I value more than all the genius in the world? Kindness and simplicity. My ambition from now on is to be just a good fellow. I know that cannot be easy, for good fellows are very rare.

To spare you any more idle talk I pass on to business matters, since you are kind enough to take charge of mine, etc.

Thank you for your good advice and the cordial interest you express. I wish I were worthy of your zeal for my welfare, but I do know that I am capable of appreciating your friendship.

Very sincerely,

PERSONAL REFLECTIONS 1847

[Ten years have elapsed between the preceding letters and the notes here jotted down in George Sand's scrapbook. The following fragment once more illustrates that when she felt ill and depressed she turned to her journal for solace, rather than burden her friends. Writing helped her to get rid of a bad mood.]

May 7, 1847.

At last, thank God, my exhausted spirit has recovered a little strength and a few days of release from strain.

The illness that consumed my energy has disappeared. To think that an intelligent physician might have helped me ten years ago! By advising the right diet he might have rid me of the accumulated bile which was burning up my liver. No matter. I probably wouldn't have had the common sense and patience to submit to the diet. For this I seem to have waited until one of my best friends became a skilled physician. Then friendship made me accept science.

Well, here I am at forty-three with iron health, impaired at times by painful attacks of illness. But the pain only lasts a few hours and the illness disappears in a day or two. Thank God I am cured of my gloomy misanthropy. I can stand physical suffering. I find it by no means unendurable unless it affects the mental state.

Nevertheless it is certain that this wretched liver of mine will be the cause of my death. This fate was foretold to me by one who is dead, a man who was wise in science and who understood my case.

Whether I die to-morrow or in twenty years from now seems unimportant. It would suit me very well to die this year. It would suit me even better to die this month, if Solange and Augustine [a young relative, adopted as a daughter] should be married by then.

I cannot say that I have ever loved life. I think I was born impatient to die. Ten years ago when I felt I was dying I was content to go. Indeed, the certainty of final death was the one comforting thought that sustained me. But I realized then that my soul was dying first, and I decided to keep my body in order to save my soul.

My soul is very well to-day—my body too. I am ready to go if my time has come. But, dear Lord, I do not want to die in anger, and I would rather die of almost anything than this horrid liver.

I wonder why the thought of suicide, and the desire for it, has come back to me so constantly of late. I suppose it is because I have recovered my health and am at peace again. I should like to fall asleep in this peaceful mood and never awake. After all, are we certain that the right to die is denied us? In my days of cynicism I used to regard suicide as an inalienable right. If I did not make use of my theory it was because mother-love made me feel responsible for my children.

Very soon now they will have no further need of me. Who knows whether my death might not benefit them more than my life?

I have always believed in God, but there was a time when I ceased to love him. Now that my concept has changed and God appears to me as infinite goodness, I love him again. I want to return to the source of life and be reborn with opportunity to grow into a better soul. But if I took my own life before completing my allotted days on earth, might not the life I had tried to dispose of be thrown back into nothingness?

God punishes and compensates. He does not judge according to man's law. He gives us no death penalties and no life sentences. Nevertheless it is my conviction that in his own way he does compensate and punish.

I am not afraid of nothingness. It seems restful. And rest is pleasant, and so desirable. But it is not important what I fear or desire in the so-called other life.

The one thing important is merging with God, who is goodness and love. Oh, enlighten me, infinite light! Why has death always seemed to me so beautiful? Why has death smiled at me since I was a little child?

May 7, 1847.

The truth is, I am just as unhappy as I have always been, and I feel unhappiness as intensely as ever. The only difference is that I have stopped complaining about it to God and man. I no longer rebel. I no longer believe that heaven is insensible nor that man is incurably perverse. I have ceased to be in conflict with myself.

As far as I could do so, I have paid for everything, made up for everything. And now I feel gentle and resigned. That does not prevent me from suffering, but it does prevent my suffering from becoming bitter and harmful to others. God has done for me all it i possible to do for a creature like me. To explain and justify him is beyond our power. He is the living law, and that law condemns us to suffer.

[At this stage of her literary development, George Sand no longer considered fame and wealth. Although she was burdened by debt and could easily have made money by writing love stories in her early vein, she decided that the mission of art was to serve humanity, which she tried to do in *Le Compagnon du Tour de France* by presenting a sympathetic study of the working class.

This so-called socialist novel was the source of serious disagreement between George and Buloz. He reluctantly accepted it as a serial for his magazine but refused to publish it afterward, so George herself had it printed in book form. *Le Compagnon* was the last George Sand novel accepted by Buloz for seventeen years (with the exception of *L'Homme de Neige,* which was sold to the magazine by an intermediary). Buloz considered George's theories "subversive," but she continued to use each new novel, much as Upton Sinclair is doing to-day, as a vehicle for radical thought and social reform.

The appearance of *Le Compagnon du Tour de France* brought down on George's obstinate head a storm of criticism. Her critics and the general public agreed that no carpenter so ideal as her hero had ever existed in this world, and that he could not appear for two or three hundred years. George was not disturbed by this dismal prophecy. She knew that "in spite of all the obstacles to his development that exist in laws, prejudices and customs, a proletarian will become a fully developed man within a few years."

So it proved, for the labor movement in France was taking root and soon began to organize. Also, a few years later in France there sprang from the working class a number of poets and writers, while a studio for artisan artists was opened in Paris. This trend toward art for the workers was held in horror by the unknown correspondent who wrote George Sand the accompanying anonymous letter. So emotional was his resistance to the temptations of art, that one sees the man as himself endowed with the creative impulse, the expression of which he regarded as treason to his class.

Why did art symbolize to him a struggle between desire and conscience? He might have been an artist. He might have been able to write a book like *Le Compagnon du Tour de France*. In any case, he seems to have been the educated, intelligent worker in whose existence the critics refused to believe.]

AN ANONYMOUS LETTER SENT TO GEORGE SAND
AFTER THE PUBLICATION OF
LE COMPAGNON DU TOUR DE FRANCE

This handwriting is unknown to you, Madame, but be good enough to go on reading, for although I am only an obscure work-ingman I would like to talk to you. Not that I aspire to be one of those who are happy enough to approach you. Such a privilege is reserved for others. In lifting my eyes to the high position you occupy, I do not expect you to lower yours to the humble place occupied by me.

But, Madame, if I respect the barrier which separates us, is there any harm in addressing you? Since you are wealthy and beautiful, distinguished and famous, I do not doubt that ambition and vanity have long ago lost their allure for you. Probably you are bored by arrogant advances and importunate homage. Nevertheless I have not restrained my impulse to write to you, because, upon reflection, I realize that this letter will cause you no surprise. The possession of intelligence gives one the power to discriminate. I cannot be deceived. I know you for what you are.

May a man who has always abstained from indiscreet adoration and who is especially respectful toward you—may such a man be permitted to say to you, Madame, that you seem to him an angel?

You have come into the desolate lives of the workers and you bring us so much sweetness and grace that you have won our hearts. Many of us are well informed in the history of our class, and as far back as history carries us, not one of us can recall the advent in our midst of a nobler, more serene soul than yours.

The children of the people have therefore become your children. Your maternal heart adopts them, and your love, as precious as it was unhoped for, puts at their service a voice whose kindness consoles them, a genius whose power defends them. Who sends you and whence do you come? You who scarcely know us, you whose sympathy overwhelms us, how shall we express our gratitude to God for you?

Suspicious and malicious people declare that your inspiration is derived from art, and somewhere you have spoken of yourself as an artist. Ah, Madame, do not slander yourself! There are plenty of others to do that for you. Allow us to believe otherwise. Your feet would never have led you to us along the muddy byways of art. At least that is what I say to my brothers when I talk of you, and I would not hesitate to say it to you yourself. And my brothers believe me because they know that I have grown old at my daily job, debating this subject. For a long time I have questioned whether the sons of the people should prepare for their enfranchisement by that devotion to art which is so recommended by the false prophets of to-day. In spite of temptations to follow art, conscience has restrained me, and I have emerged from this dangerous experience free enough to advise those about me not to eat stones offered in the place of bread.

If nevertheless, Madame, you believe you have come to us across the fields of art, may you still be blessed, may you always be loved! May you be loved even more, if possible, for your feeling, your light, and your devotion, if they have been saved to us out of that source of vanity and egotism where all goodness grows embittered, all feeling goes astray, and all light is extinguished.

Good-by, Madame, and for the sake of your peace and quiet, bear in mind that if the world's unkindness sometimes seeks you out, the people's gratitude always follows and finds you. It is yours forever.

Among philosophers and artists you alone—who are, I insist, neither the one nor the other, although wisdom and inspiration have made you very great—you alone will find arms to defend you in the days of coming danger, from which may God protect you. And on the day of your death—which day may God delay— the hearts of the workers who love you will be torn by grief.

May your children crown you with love and pride, may your old age be productive, your sleep restful, your life happy, and your glory everlasting!

Note by George Sand:

(The only letter of the kind that ever gave me pleasure. A hundred other letters have resembled it in content. None has shown this spirit, which touched me deeply. I never knew who wrote it. Unknown friend, I thank you.)

GEORGE SAND DEFINES HAPPINESS

1852.

The consciousness of self as animal, vegetable and mineral, and the delight we feel in plunging down into that consciousness, is by no means degrading. It is good to know the fundamental life at our roots, while we reach out toward that higher life which is completely attained only in flashes of insight and in dreams.

In striving for truth and happiness we should not allow ourselves to regard these two goals of human effort as illusions. When we struggle for truth we find a part of it. When we dream of happiness it is already ours.

The satisfaction of a personal passion is pleasure or intoxication. It is not happiness.

Happiness, to deserve the name, must be enduring and indestructible. Those who try to find happiness in excitement attempt the impossible. The highest form of excitement is exaltation, a state so exceptional that if persisted in, it would end in killing us. A nervous system completely abandoned to transports of emotion would burst asunder.

Spring means fever. Autumn means repose. Late autumn leads slowly to mistiness and sleep. Maturity loves quiet and accepts it as an expression of happiness. In youth, happiness is still unrealized and unsought. Youth prefers joy, exhilaration, the sense of power.

When we are young it is enough to feel alive, which is always possible under normal conditions; it is enough to live fully, take risks, know the price of experience and accept the consequences. To live thus is to believe in life.

Maturity finds happiness in a state of grace, that is, the consciousness of good behind one, before one, and within one. The capacity for such happiness shows complete absence of mean motives. In the state of grace one cannot bear to give pain or do injury. One need not be a saint or a great man, nor even pose as virtuous in order to attain this state of being. It is within reach of everyone.

I deny that there is any happiness in wealth.

But I have been dwelling on individual happiness. I submit that it is incomplete. Complete happiness requires the general happiness of society. Without this vicarious quality it is so fragmentary, so personal, that it scarcely exists and cannot be accurately defined.

The happiness of others is absolutely necessary to our own. Opinions to the contrary must be boldly fought. On the other hand, there is a certain type of socialist who exaggerates this aspect of the question. One need not go so far as M. Montigut, who sees social happiness as the only thing worth striving for. He believes that the Blanqui Club is the goal of this aspiration for social happiness.

The error of socialism, thus understood, is that it overlooks the importance of the individual. It hopes to impose the happiness of all on each. It is true that justice and liberty will make room for more individual satisfactions. But we cannot hand out happiness to others. The individual must win his own. Violence destroys happiness, whereas time and education will develop men and women until they find their own happiness in harmony with social well-being.

FINAL COMMENT BY GEORGE SAND

September, 1868.

I HAPPENED to reread all this. I must have been quite in love with this book. I intended to fill it with beautiful things. But I have written nothing but foolishness. That is very evident to me to-day.

My plan in jotting down these thoughts and feelings was based on a theory I once believed in. I used to imagine that I could pick up my own identity from time to time and carry it on. Can one thus resume one's self? Can one know one's self? Is one ever *somebody?* I don't know anything about it any more. It now seems to me that one changes from day to day and that every few years one becomes a new being. It is useless to search for my former identity. I fail to find within me any trace of that anxious, agitated person who was dissatisfied with herself and impatient of others. No doubt I cherished the illusion of greatness. It was the fashion in those days. We all wanted to be great, and if we failed in this, we fell into despair. I see now that goodness and sincerity were quite enough for me to undertake.

And now I am very old, gently traversing my sixty-fifth year. By some freak of destiny I am stronger and more active than I was in youth. I can walk farther. I can stay awake longer. My body has remained as supple as a glove. My sight is somewhat blurred, so that I have to wear spectacles, but they have increased my interest in natural history, as they enable me to see in the grass and sand tiny objects I might have overlooked. I go in bathing in icy water and find it pleasant. I never catch cold, and I have forgotten what rheumatism is. I am absolutely calm. My old age is as chaste in thought as it is in deed. I have no regret for youth, no ambition for fame, and no desire for money, except that I would like to have a little to leave to my children and grandchildren. I have no complaints to make of my friends. My one sorrow is that humanity does not go forward fast enough. Society seems indifferent to progress. But who knows what this lethargy conceals? What awakening may be latent in this torpor?

I no longer live in myself. My heart has gone into my children and my friends. I suffer only through their sufferings. However, that means that I suffer a good deal, sometimes too much, because considerable energy is needed to bear up under their burdens. I lack the courage necessary for meeting other people's troubles. If there were no other people in existence I should, therefore, be perfectly happy—happy, that is, as a stone, if one could imagine a stone capable of looking on at life—but other people do exist and through them I live. I rejoice with them and I grieve with them.

I have no more needs for myself. Shall I live much longer? Is this astonishing old age without infirmity and without weariness a sign of long life? Or shall I drop off suddenly? No use wondering. One may be snatched away by an accident any moment. Shall I keep on being useful? Ah, that is worth wondering about. It seems to me that I shall. I feel that my service is more personal, more direct than ever. I have acquired considerable wisdom without knowing where it came from. I could bring up children much better than I once could.

I remain a believer, a believer in God—the life eternal—evil some day vanquished by science, science illumined by love. But symbols, images, cults, human gods?—good-by! I have passed beyond all that.

I have become impersonal, universal, that is all. And, since I can bear the evil in my life and appreciate the good, I am not in the least interesting. May those whom I love outlive me! I cannot imagine what would become of me without my family at Nohant. I care very little about living on. Death is kind and gentle. My only dread of death is in the thought of the grief it would cause my loved ones.

Have I been useful to them these last twenty years? I believe so. I have earnestly wanted to be. So I was wrong when I used to imagine that there are crises in life when one may hand in one's resignation without injury to others. Because here I am, still useful at an advanced age. My brain has not failed. Indeed, I feel that it has acquired a great deal, and that it is better nourished than it ever was.

It is a mistake to regard age as a downhill grade toward dissolution. The reverse is true. As one grows older one climbs with surprising strides. Mental activity increases with age, as physical activity develops in a child. Meanwhile, and nevertheless, one approaches the journey's end. But the end is a goal, not a catastrophe.

GEORGE SAND

IMPORTANT DATES AND EVENTS IN THE LIFE OF
GEORGE SAND

1804 George Sand, daughter of Maurice Dupin and Sophie Delaborde, is born July 1st at 15 Rue de la Meslay, Paris. She is christened Amandine Aurore Lucie Dupin.

   The Dupins move to a humble apartment, Rue de la Grange-Batelière, Paris.

1808 Sophie Dupin and Aurore travel to Madrid, Spain. They live at the Palace de Goday, where Maurice Dupin is stationed under General Murat of Napoleon's army.

1809 Aurore travels with her parents to Nohant, France, the home of her paternal grandmother, Madame Dupin (Marie-Aurore de Saxe, Comtesse de Horn), the daughter of Marshal Saxe, who was the natural son of King Frederic-Augustus II of Poland.

   Maurice Dupin is killed by a fall from his horse.

1810 Plebeian Sophie Dupin, pensioned by Madame Dupin, consents to surrender her daughter Aurore to the child's aristocratic grandmother.

1810–1814 Aurore spends her winters at Paris in her grandmother's apartment, Rue Neuve-des-Mathurins, where she is allowed to see her mother. Her summers are spent at Nohant.

1814–1817 Winters and summers are spent at Nohant. Consumed by loneliness for her absent mother, Aurore is indifferent to the teaching of her father's ex-tutor, Deschartres.

1817–1820   Aurore is educated at the English Convent des Augustines in Paris. Disillusioned with her mother, she longs to become a nun.

1820   Aurore is isolated at Nohant with the two old people, Deschartres and Madame Dupin. She studies and practices medicine with Deschartres.

1821   Death of Madame Dupin, whose will makes Aurore heiress of a small fortune and owner of a house in Paris and the Nohant estate.

Forbidden to stay at Nohant alone, Aurore lives unhappily with her alienated mother at 80 Rue St.-Lazare, Paris.

1822   She visits the Duplessis family at Plessis-Picard near Melun, where she meets the ex-soldier, Casimir Dudevant.

September 10th Aurore is married to Casimir Dudevant, son of Baron Dudevant, retired Colonel of the Empire. The young couple live in the wife's home at Nohant.

1823   They visit Paris. On June 30 Aurore Dudevant's son Maurice is born at Hotel de Florence, 56 Rue Neuve-des-Mathurins.

1824   Dreading the tête-à-tête solitude of their country home, the Dudevants spend the spring and summer with the Duplessis, the autumn at Ormesson, a suburb of Paris, and the winter in a Paris apartment, Rue du Faubourg-Saint-Honoré.

1825   Spring finds them again at Nohant. The young wife, neglected by her husband, suffers from ill health. During the summer Madame Dudevant's ill health becomes serious. Change of scene is recommended. She travels with her husband to the home of his family at Guillery in Gascony. During the journey south she meets Aurélian de Sèze and recovers her health.

On November 5th Madame Dudevant writes her famous eighteen-page confession to her husband, asking his permission to keep Sèze as her friend. The winter is spent at Guillery. Madame Dudevant sacrifices love to duty. Casimir promises to console her loneliness by his companionship.

1826   Madame Dudevant lives at Nohant. Casimir travels on business, while his wife manages the estate and composes long letters to Aurélian de Sèze.

1827   Illness again necessitates change of scene. She visits the water cure Clermont-Ferraud, where she writes a brief autobiography entitled *Voyage en Auvergne*. This is her first literary effort.

1827–1829   The Dudevants winter at La Châtre and summer at Nohant.

1828   September 13th. Birth of a daughter, Solange.

1829   Jules Boucoiran is engaged as tutor for young Maurice.

1830   Madame Dudevant visits Bordeaux, the home of Aurélian de Sèze. She finds he is weary of Platonic love. Their correspondence ceases. She writes a novel, entitled *Aimée*.

December, she finds Casimir's will, expressing hatred for his wife.

1831   On January 4th Madame Dudevant departs for Paris, where she lives for a time at her half-brother's apartment, 31 Rue de Seine. She joins the staff of the *Figaro* and publishes three short stories, *La Molinara* (*Le Figaro*); *La Prima Donna* (*Revue de Paris*); *La Fille d'Albano* (*La Mode*).

April she returns to Nohant for a three months'

visit with her children. At Nohant she writes *Indiana*.

July she moves to 25 Quai Saint-Michel, Paris.

September and October. Nohant.

November and December. Paris.

In December is published *Rose et Blanche*, a collaboration by Aurore Dudevant and Jules Sandeau. The novel is signed Jules Sand.

1832   She continues to travel back and forth between Nohant and Paris.

April, Solange is brought to Paris and in November is established with her mother at 19 Quai Malaquais.

Indiana and *Valentine* are published.

Maurice is sent by his father to the Henry IV Military Academy in Paris.

1833   January. George breaks with Sandeau.

June. She meets Alfred de Musset.

During the summer *Lélia* is published.

September. She visits Fontainebleau with Alfred de Musset.

December 12. Sand and Musset depart for Italy.

1834   January 19. They reach Venice and stay at the Hotel Danieli. Musset tells George he has ceased to love her.

Musset is seriously ill. His physician is Dr. Pietro Pagello. His nurse is George Sand. Physician and nurse fall in love. March 29, Musset returns to Paris.

In Venice during five months George Sand writes *André, Mattéa, Jacques, Léone Léoni*, and the first of the *Lettres d'un Voyageur*.

August 15, Sand and Pagello reach Paris. August 25, Musset departs for Baden. August 29, Sand goes to Nohant, where she stays about a month. Early in

October Sand is in Paris. Musset returns from Baden October 13. Pagello returns to Venice October 23.

November 25th. George Sand begins her journal to Alfred de Musset.

December. She goes to Nohant and tries in vain to forget Musset. A month later she is back in Paris.

1835   March 6th occurs the final break with Musset.

Six weeks later George meets Michel of Bourges, who becomes her lawyer and advises against legal separation from Casimir. She goes to Paris and enters politics under the guidance of Michel. She writes *Simon.*

In the autumn George returns to Nohant for Maurice's vacation.

October 19th, Casimir threatens his wife with a gun. She begins suit for legal separation. December 1st, a judgment in favor of Madame Dudevant is won by default.

1836   February 16th, a second judgment is won by Madame Dudevant. Casimir, who has agreed not to contest, now brings counter suit.

On May 10th and 11th the case is tried in the civil court of La Châtre. Verdict is in favor of Madame Dudevant. Casimir appeals to the higher court.

July 25 and 26. Trial in the royal court of Bourges. The jury is divided and a new trial is announced. The case is finally settled out of court. Madame Dudevant divides her fortune with her husband. The legal adjustments continue for another year.

In August Madame Sand, with her two children, goes to Chamonix and Geneva, Switzerland, where she stays with Franz Liszt and Madame d'Agoult.

In the autumn the three friends reside at the Hotel

de la France, 15 Rue Lafitte, Paris. At this time Madame Sand meets Frederic Chopin at an informal gathering in his apartment.

1837   In January Madame Sand returns to Nohant where she spends the winter completing *Mauprat*. In the spring *Mauprat* is published. She writes *Les Maîtres Mosaïstes*. During June and July Franz Liszt and Madame d'Agoult visit Nohant. Their visit is terminated by the fatal illness of George Sand's mother. George goes to Paris, then to Fontainebleau, where she writes *La Dernière Aldini*. Later she hastens to Guillery to recover the kidnapped Solange.

1838   She writes two Venetian novels, *l'Orco* and *l'Uscoque*.

In May Madame Sand goes to Paris where her friendship with Chopin develops into romance.

In November Sand and Chopin, with Maurice and Solange, visit Majorca. During their stay on the island, George completes the religious anti-orthodox novel *Spiridion*.

1839   In February they leave Majorca and spend three months in Marseilles. From Marseilles they go to Nohant where they remain until October.

George Sand publishes *Un Hiver à Majorque, Pauline* and *Gabriel-Gabrielle*. From October, 1839, until the spring of 1841 Sand and Chopin occupy adjoining apartments at 16 Rue Pigalle, Paris, during the winter. The summers, from 1839 to 1847 (excepting the summer of 1840) are spent at Nohant, where Chopin is an honored guest.

1840   George Sand writes *Compagnon du Tour de France* and *Horace*. These and other novels of social reform are influenced by the visionary philosopher, Pierre Leroux.

1841   Sand and Chopin leave Rue Pigalle for 5 and 9 Rue St.-Lazare, Square d'Orléans. Their mutual friend, Madame Marliani, occupies the intervening apartment.

1842   *Consuelo* is a literary sensation.

1843   *Consuelo* is continued by *La Comtesse de Rudolstadt.*

1844   In her literary evolution George Sand has now outgrown romanticism. *Jeanne* foreshadows her great pastoral novels.

1845   *Tévérino,* the story of a vagabond.
Péché de M. Antoine, socialist novel.
Le Meunier d'Angibault, socialist novel.

1846   *La Mare au Diable,* pastoral novel. *Lucrezia Floriani,* psychological study of the artistic temperament. Marriage of Solange to the sculptor, Auguste-Jean Clésinger. Estrangement of Sand and Chopin. George abandons the search for happiness.

1847   *François le Champi,* pastoral novel.

1848   George Sand lends her pen to the Second Republic. She writes government circulars, contributes to the *Bulletins de la République,* and publishes her own newspaper, *La Cause du Peuple.*

Death of George Sand's first grandchild, the son of Solange.

La Petite Fadette, pastoral novel.

1849   George Sand's dramatic adaptation of her novel, *François le Champi,* is presented at the Odéon. This is the first of a series of successful plays produced in the leading theaters of Paris. Of these plays *Claudie* (1851) and *Le Pressoir* (1853) are rustic dramas. Two society comedies, *Le Mariage de Victorine* (1851) and *Le Marquis de Villemer* (1864), give her more enduring fame as a playwright.

1850   *Château des Désertes* is published in the *Revue des Deux Mondes.*

1851   After the fall of the Republic George Sand spends several months in Paris, where she uses her influence with Prince President Napoleon to save her Republican friends from exile and death.

1852   George returns to Nohant.

1853   *Les Maîtres Sonneurs,* pastoral novel.

1855   She publishes her four-volume autobiography, *L'Histoire de ma Vie,* which carries her life story up to the Revolution of 1848.

   January 13. Death of Jeanne Clésinger, George Sand's adored grandchild. February. George visits Italy, accompanied by her son Maurice and her friend Alexandre Manceau.

1856   She adapts Shakespeare's *As You Like It* for the French stage.

1858   She begins to spend her vacations at Gargilesse on the river Creuse, where her cottage is the gift of Alexandre Manceau.

1859   She writes *Elle et Lui,* and publishes *Jean de la Roche* and *L'Homme de Neige.*

1860   *La Ville Noire* and *Marquis de Villemer.*

   In November George has typhoid fever. From February until June she visits Tamaris near Toulon.

1862   May 16. Marriage of Maurice Sand and Caroline ("Lina") Calamatta, daughter of Luigi Calamatta.

1863   July 14. Birth of a grandchild, Marc-Antoine Sand, the son of Maurice and Lina.

   Publication of *Mademoiselle La Quintinie,* censored as a play in 1872. This anti-clerical novel creates a storm of protest and gives to George the name of heretic.

George Sand begins her old-age friendship with Gustave Flaubert.

1864   Sensational success of the dramatization of *Marquis de Villemer*.

Death of the third grandchild, Marc-Antoine.

During the period of her fame as a playwright George Sand lived at 3 Rue Racine, near the Odéon, where she was surrounded by men and women of the theater. She now moves to 97 Rue des Feuillantines, and Gargilesse is exchanged for a country place at Palaiseau, where she lives with Manceau.

1865   Death of Manceau. For a year she continues to live at Palaiseau alone.

1866   She visits Flaubert at Croisset and dedicates to him *Le Dernier Amour*.

Birth of Aurore Sand, the fourth and favorite grandchild.

1867   After a severe illness George returns to Nohant to live with her son Maurice. She now devotes herself to her son's family, interests herself in the study of natural history, is surrounded by friends, and is revered as "The Good Lady of Nohant." She continues to write two novels a year.

1868   Birth of a fifth grandchild, Gabrielle Sand.

1869   George Sand reckons that she has made $200,000 by her writings, of which almost nothing remains.

1870   The play *L'Autre*, acted at the Théâtre Français by Sarah Bernhardt, is a notable stage success.

1870–1871   George nurses Maurice through typhoid fever, endures the horrors of the Franco-German war, accompanies her family to Boussac in order to escape smallpox, and sustains her friends by her faith that a Republic will save France.

1876   On June 8th, at the age of seventy-two, George Sand dies at Nohant, leaving a host of friends, and, especially in the writing profession, a few bitter enemies.

Beginning in 1836 and continuing through 1840 appears the first edition of George Sand's works, published by Bonnaire in 24 volumes.

A second edition of George Sand's works, begun by Perrotin, who published 16 volumes between 1842-1844, is continued in 1847 by Garnier.

A third incomplete edition of George Sand's works, with illustrations by Maurice Sand, is published by Hetzel between 1851-1856.

The fourth edition of George Sand's works, undertaken by Hetzel and Lecou in 1852, is continued by Michel Lévy through 77 volumes. The fifth edition by Calmann Lévy comprises 112 volumes.